UEHIRO SERIES IN PRAC⸍
General Editor: Julian Savulescu, ˈ

Unfit for the Future

UEHIRO SERIES IN PRACTICAL ETHICS

General Editor: Julian Savulescu, University of Oxford

Choosing Children
Genes, Disability, and Design
Jonathan Glover

Messy Morality
The Challenge of Politics
C. A. J. Coady

Killing in War
Jeff McMahan

Ethics for Enemies
Terror, Torture, and War
F. M. Kamm

Beyond Humanity?
The Ethics of Biomedical Enhancement
Allen Buchanan

Unfit for the Future
The Need for Moral Enhancement
Ingmar Persson & Julian Savulescu

Unfit for the Future

The Need for Moral Enhancement

Ingmar Persson & Julian Savulescu

OXFORD
UNIVERSITY PRESS

OXFORD
UNIVERSITY PRESS

Great Clarendon Street, Oxford OX2 6DP
United Kingdom

Oxford University Press is a department of the University of Oxford.
It furthers the University's objective of excellence in research, scholarship,
and education by publishing worldwide. Oxford is a registered trade mark of
Oxford University Press in the UK and in certain other countries

First Edition published in 2012
First published in paperback 2014

Published in the United States of America by Oxford University Press
198 Madison Avenue, New York, NY 10016, United States of America

British Library Cataloguing in Publication Data
Data available

Library of Congress Cataloging in Publication Data
Data available

ISBN 978–0–19–965364–5 (Hbk)
ISBN 978–0–19–870792–9 (Pbk)

The Uehiro Series in Practical Ethics

In 2002, the Uehiro Foundation on Ethics and Education, chaired by Mr Eiji Uehiro, established the Uehiro Chair in Practical Ethics at the University of Oxford. The following year, the Oxford Uehiro Centre for Practical Ethics was created within the Faculty of Philosophy. Generous support by the Uehiro Foundation enabled the establishment of an annual series of three lectures, the Uehiro Lectures in Practical Ethics.

The Uehiro Lectures, given each year in Oxford, capture the ethos of the Oxford Uehiro Centre for Practical Ethics: their goal is to foster debate and deeper rational reflection on practical ethics. It is not to promote a particular philosophy, approach, solution, or truth, though often an argument to a substantive conclusion will be made to provide a basis for dialogue, engagement, and reflection. It is the method of rational analytic practical ethics that we aim to advance, not firm conclusions to problems in practical ethics, which is an evolving, rich, and complex discipline. The vision is Socratic, not missionary. Philosophy should not only create knowledge, it should make people's lives better. We aim to do this by promoting open, deeper, rational, ethical reflection and dialogue.

The Uehiro Series in Practical Ethics has been established for the publication of books that further these aims, mostly derived from the Uehiro Lectures. This volume discusses why and how people's moral dispositions should be enhanced if we are to address some of the most profound issues of the century.

Julian Savulescu
Uehiro Chair in Practical Ethics
Director, Oxford Uehiro Centre for Practical Ethics, University of Oxford
Editor, The Uehiro Series in Practical Ethics

Contents

Acknowledgements

We would both like to first express our deep gratitude and appreciation for the wide-ranging, long, and deep support of the Uehiro Foundation of Ethics and Education for making this book possible, in so many ways.

We would like to thank audiences at the Universities of Tokyo, Melbourne, Granada, Barcelona, Oxford, Princeton, Stockholm, Gothenburg, Belgrade, Belo Horizonte, as well as Federal University of Rio De Janeiro. Work related to this book was also presented in the Crown Lecture at Duke, and in the Fulvio Guerrini Lecture, at the Sydney Dangerous Ideas Festival, at a Brocher Foundation conference, and at the International Association of Bioethics World Congress. Related material was also presented at a 'Necker Meets Oxford' and a Consilium event, as well as at the Australian Leaders Retreat, the World Economic Forum, the Adelaide Festival of Ideas, the BBC Radio 3 Free Thinking Festival, and the 2011 Carnegie- Uehiro-Oxford Conference on Shaping Moral Psychology. We would like to thank all these audiences for valuable questions and suggestions.

Material related to this book has appeared in podcast form:

Adelaide Festival of Ideas: http://radio.adelaide.edu.au/adelaidefestivalofideas2011/audio/08_perfection.mp3

BBC Free Thinking Festival: http://www.bbc.co.uk/programmes/b01757kg

Sydney Slow TV: http://www.themonthly.com.au/genetically-enhance-humanity-or-face-extinction-julian-savulescu-2065

http://www.sandford.duke.edu/images/mmfeatures/savulescu_ref.mov

Crown Lectures: http://www.rsssearchhub.com/preview/podcasts-from-the-uehiro-centre-for-practical-ethics-rss-rrpmrp/

Parts of this book began as work in the following papers:

Persson, I. and Savulescu, J. (2008) 'The Perils of Cognitive Enhancement and the Urgent Imperative to Enhance the Moral Character of Humanity', *Journal of Applied Philosophy* 25: 162–76.

Persson, I. and Savulescu, J. (2010) 'Moral Transhumanism', *Journal of Medicine and Philosophy* 35: 656–69. Thematic Issue on Transhumanism and Bioethics. http://jmp.oxfordjournals.org/content/early/2010/11/12/jmp.jhq052.full

Persson, I. and Savulescu, J. (2011) 'The Turn for Ultimate Harm: A Reply to Fenton', *Journal of Medical Ethics* 37: 441–4.

Persson, I. and Savulescu, J. (2011) 'Unfit for the Future? Human Nature, Scientific Progress and the Need for Moral Enhancement', in J. Savulescu, R. Ter Meulen, and G. Kahane (eds.), *Enhancing Human Capacities*. Oxford: Wiley-Blackwell.

Persson, I. and Savulescu, J. (2011) 'Getting Moral Enhancement Right: The Desirability of Moral Enhancement', *Bioethics* 27: 124–131.

We are especially grateful to Thomas Douglas for working with us on the project on moral enhancement. His doctorate on this topic provided an important impetus for our thinking about this book. Many thanks also to Allen Buchanan, Peter Momtchiloff, and three anonymous OUP readers for valuable comments on earlier drafts.

We would like to thank those who have reviewed or edited these papers for their comments which were invaluable in developing our ideas, especially John Harris who has responded to some of our articles.

Arts & Humanities Research Council

Research related to this work has also been supported by Wellcome Trust [086041/Z/08/Z], Arts and Humanities Research Council [AH/F019513] and Oxford Martin School (Institute for Science and Ethics).

Since the publication of the hardback edition of this book, we have responded to commentators and published on matters related to it as follows:

1. Savulescu, J. and Maslen, H. 'Moral Enhancement and Artificial Intelligence: Moral AI?', in Jan Romportl, Eva Zackova, Jozef Kelemen (eds.), *'Beyond Artificial Intelligence: The Disappearing Human-Machine Divide'*, *Topics in Intelligent Engineering and Informatics*, pp. 66–82.

2. Savulescu, J., Persson, I., and Douglas, T. (2014) 'Autonomy and the Ethics of Behavioural Modification', in Akira Akabayashi (ed.), *The*

Future of Bioethics: International Dialogues. Oxford: Oxford University Press, pp. 91–112.

3. Persson, I. and Savulescu, J., (forthcoming). The Art of Misunderstanding Moral Bioenhancement: Two Cases. *Cambridge Quarterly of Health Care Ethics*.

4. Savulescu, J. and Harris, J. (forthcoming) 'A Debate About Moral Enhancement', *Cambridge Quarterly of Health Care Ethics*.

5. Savulescu, J. and Persson I. (forthcoming 2014) 'Against Fetishism about Egalitarianism and In Defence of Cautious Moral Bioenhancement', *American Journal of Bioethics*.

6. Persson, I. and Savulescu, J. (forthcoming 2014) 'Unfit for the Future: Reply to Commentators', *Journal of Medical Ethics*. Online first December 2013.

7. Schaefer, O., Kahane, G., and Savulescu, J. (forthcoming), 'Autonomy and Enhancement', *Neuroethics*.

8. Douglas, T., Kahane, G., Levy, N., and Savulescu, J. (order TBC), 'Disease, Normality and Current Pharmacological Moral Modification', *Philosophy, Psychology, Psychiatry*.

9. Persson I., and Savulescu J. (2013) 'Should Moral Bioenhancement Be Compulsory? Reply to Vojin Rakic' (Commentary), *Journal of Medical Ethics*.

10. Persson, I. and Savulescu, J. (forthcoming) 'Summary of *Unfit for the Future*', *Journal of Medical Ethics*. Online first December 2013.

11. Kahane, G. and Savulescu, J. (2013) 'Normal Variation: Refocusing the Enhancement Debate', *Bioethics*. DOI: 10.1111/bioe.12045.

12. Kahane, G. and Savulescu, J. (2012) 'The Concept of Harm and the Significance of Normality', *Journal of Applied Philosophy* 29(4): 318–332.

13. Levy, N., Douglas, T., Kahane, G., Terbeck, S., Cowen, P, Hewstone, M. and Savulescu, J. (forthcoming) 'Are You Morally Modified? The Moral Effects of Widely Used Pharmaceuticals', *Philosophy, Psychiatry and Psychology*.

14. Terbeck, S., Kahane, G., McTavish, S., Savulescu, J., Cowen, P. and Hewstone, M. (2012) 'Propranolol reduces implicit negative racial bias', *Psychopharmacology* 222(3): 419–24.

15. Savulescu, J. and Persson, I. (2012) 'Moral Enhancement, Freedom and the God Machine,' *The Monist* 95:3, 399–421.
16. Kahane, G., Wiech, K., Shackel, N., Farias, M., Savulescu, J. and Tracey, I. (2011) 'The Neural Basis of Intuitive and Counterintuitive Moral Judgement', *Social, Cognitive and Affective Neuroscience*. Published online March. Forthcoming in print. doi: 10.1093.
17. Persson, I. and Savulescu, J. (2012) 'Moral Enhancement', *Philosophy Now*, Issue 91.
18. Persson, I. (2012) 'Could it be permissible to prevent the existence of morally enhanced people?', *Journal of Medical Ethics* 38: 638–9.
19. Persson, I. (2013) 'Is Agar Biased Against Post-Persons?', *Journal of Medical Ethics* 39: 77–8.

Oxford, April 2014
IP & JS

1

Introduction

For most of the 150,000 years or so that the human species has existed, human beings have lived in comparatively small and close-knit societies, with a primitive technology that allowed them to affect only their most immediate environment. So, their psychology and morality are likely to be adapted to make them fit to live in these conditions. But by science and technology humans have radically changed their living conditions, while their moral psychology has presumably remained fundamentally the same throughout this change, since the change has occurred relatively rapidly (on an evolutionary timescale), especially in the last centuries. The human population on Earth has increased a thousand times since the agricultural revolution, so most humans now live in societies with millions of people, with an advanced scientific technology that enables them to exercise an influence that extends all over the world and far into the future. We shall argue that human beings are not by nature equipped with a moral psychology that empowers them to cope with the moral problems that these new conditions of life create. Nor could the currently favoured political system of liberal democracy overcome these moral deficiencies. In fact, we shall argue that liberal democracy rather makes some of these problems more acute.

In particular, we shall look at two problems generated by the existence of modern scientific technology: the threats of weapons of mass destruction, especially in the hands of terrorist groups, and of climate change and environmental degradation. We believe that in order to come to grips with the risk of terrorist attacks with weapons of mass destruction liberal democracies will have to become less liberal, by intensifying the surveillance of their citizens and, thus, curtailing their right to privacy. But it will probably prove even harder for liberal democracies to tackle the problem of climate change and environmental destruction, for in order to do so a majority of their voters must support the adoption of substantial restrictions on their excessively consumerist lifestyle, and there is no indication that they would be willing to make such sacrifices of personal welfare in order to promote the interests of future generations and non-human animals.

We shall contend that in order for the majority of citizens of liberal democracies to be willing to go along with constraints on their extravagant consumption, their moral motivation must be enhanced so that they pay more heed to the interests of future generations and non-human animals. This could be done partly by the traditional methods of moral education, e.g. by regular reflection on the grounds or reasons that make actions morally right, and by vivid representation of what it could feel like to be at the receiving end of wrongful actions. But our knowledge of human biology, in particular of genetics and neurobiology, is now beginning to supply us with means of directly affecting the biological or physiological bases of human motivation, e.g. by the use of pharmacological and genetic methods, like genetic selection and engineering. We shall suggest that there are in principle no philosophical or moral objections to the use of such biomedical means of moral enhancement—*moral bioenhancement*, as we shall call it—and that the current predicament of humankind is so serious that it is imperative that scientific research explore every possibility of developing effective means of moral bioenhancement, as a complement to traditional means. The current predicament of humankind is most serious because human beings now have at their disposal means by which they could undermine the conditions of worthwhile life on Earth *forever*. For instance, it might be that, as essential natural resources become depleted, this ignites a devastating nuclear war. It is desirable that only beings who are morally enlightened, and adequately informed about the relevant facts, should be entrusted with such formidable technological powers as we now possess.

It might reasonably be doubted that there is enough time for human beings to undergo the requisite degree of moral enhancement before it is too late, before they put their formidable technological powers to cata-strophic use. The moral improvement achieved by traditional methods of moral training in the 2,500 years since the first great moral teachers, e.g. Buddha, Confucius, and Socrates, appeared falls short, and effective means of moral bioenhancement are not yet in the offing. Moreover, there is a worrying bootstrapping problem: biomedical means of moral enhance-ment will have to be sought out and applied by the very people who are themselves morally inadequate and in need of enhancement. So there is a significant risk, either that there is not sufficient interest in seeking them out or, if they are sought out and found, these means would be misapplied, just as other means that science has put into human hands have been.

We shall not attempt to settle how likely it is that any such dystopian prediction about our chances of correcting the mismatch between our technological and moral capacity will turn out to be right. But in making such a judgement it is probably better to err on the optimistic than on the pessimistic side, for human beings are certainly not biologically or genetically destined or determined to do themselves in eventually by being too successful in exploiting natural resources. It is possible for them to undergo considerable moral enhancement, since more than any other animal, humans are biologically or genetically disposed to learn from experience, though it cannot be reliably predicted whether or not they will in time actualize their potential for moral improvement to the requisite degree. And given the gravity of the adverse outcome and the uncertainty that traditional means of enhancement could accomplish the great moral boost necessary, it is important to pursue research into the possibility of moral bioenhancement, and not to put aside the prospect of techniques of human moral bioenhancement as being impossible in principle or morally objectionable, though there is no guarantee that efficient techniques of this kind will be discovered in time.

In Chapter 2, we start out by noting a basic fact about the conditions of our existence—that it is easier for us to harm each other than to benefit each other. For instance, it is easier for us to kill each other than it is for us to save each other's lives, and to injure each other than to cure each other. This fact that it is easier to harm than to benefit is particularly important for the reason that, as human powers of action have increased, due to the exponential development of scientific technology, the human power to harm has been become truly overwhelming. It is now capable of forever putting an end to all worthwhile life on this planet because scientific technology has supplied us with weapons of mass destruction. It has also enabled us to exploit natural resources so efficiently that we now count 7 billion and have colonized the whole planet and overused 2/3 of its most important eco-systems (according to United Nations' *Millennium Eco-System Assessment*, 2005). The resulting predicament is the centrepiece of this book.

The fact that it is easier for us to harm than to benefit is reflected in our emotional life and morality. According to common-sense morality, or the basic everyday moral norms that regulate human behaviour across cultures, our responsibility is largely based on causation, so that we see ourselves as more responsible for an outcome, the greater our causal contribution to it is. This implies that we intuitively feel, for example, that we are more responsible for the harm we cause than for benefits we fail to cause and, thus, have moral duties or obligations not to harm, but not to benefit. These negative duties correspond to there being negative rights not to be harmed, but no positive rights to be benefited. Our greater vulnerability to harm is also reflected in the fact that our aversion to losses is greater than our attraction to comparable gains, that the negative emotion of fear can be much stronger than its positive counterpart, the emotion of hope or longing, that anger at an evildoer can be stronger than gratitude towards a benefactor, and so on.

Another important feature of our psychology is that we are personally and temporally 'myopic', disposed to care more about what happens in the near future to ourselves and some individuals who are near and dear to us than about what happens to ourselves in the more remote future and to strangers. We tend to discount the more distant future, and we are capable of empathizing and sympathizing only with a few individuals, centred around ourselves, and not with larger numbers of individuals in proportion to their number. Our readiness to engage in reciprocal cooperation, which involves a sense of justice or fairness, is also limited to the small number of people whom we care about and put trust in. Strangers, those outside the group of individuals whom we personally know, are generally met with unconcern and distrust, which the smallest offence could transform into downright hostility. These are the traits of our moral psychology that we believe to be of greatest relevance in the present context. We hypothesize that there are evolutionary explanations for them, but it is the fact that we exhibit these traits rather than their origin which is of most importance for our argument.

Chapter 3 takes a quick look at the nature of liberal democracy. By liberal democracies, we mean countries like those of the European Union, the United States of America, Canada, Australia, New Zealand, and Japan. We shall focus especially on the ability of such affluent liberal democracies to handle the mega-threats of weapons of mass destruction and environmental problems like climate change, loss of biodiversity, and depletion of essential resources like oil, water, and arable land. This is because these countries are well-equipped, economically and technologically, to deal with these problems, and most of our readers are likely to be resident in these countries.

We are not going to provide a detailed abstract characterization of what a liberal democracy is. It is, however, essential for our argument that one of the defining features of a liberal democracy is the provision to its citizens of extensive civil rights and liberties, roughly, as extensive as is compatible with all citizens having equal rights and liberties. We note in passing that, although liberal democracies uphold equality in respect of rights and liberties, they contain a considerable socio-economic inequality, which is an inevitable consequence of their market economy and the differences with respect to the natural psycho-physical talents of human beings. Thus, although liberal democracies typically have a commitment to equality, in the sense of equal rights and opportunities, this commitment does not extend to full-blooded socio-economic equality and, for this reason, is rather hollow. But to attain socio-economic equality in a market economy, it is not enough to create an equality of social opportunities. It would also take an enhancement of the intellectual and practical capacities of human beings, e.g. by means of genetic or pharmacological methods, to make humans more equal in respect of them. The focus of this book, however, is on moral enhancement, i.e. enhancement of specifically moral dispositions, rather than on enhancement of human capacities in general.

Chapter 4 reviews the catastrophic threats posed by nuclear and biological weapons of mass destruction. Nuclear weapons are comparatively difficult to manufacture, but it might be possible for a resourceful terrorist group to do so, now or in the near future. It is certainly possible for a terrorist group to produce biological weapons of mass destruction and, because they are contagious, they could be almost as lethal. We argue that to protect themselves against terrorist attacks using weapons of mass destruction, liberal democracies must employ modern technology of surveillance, such as monitoring of electromagnetic transmissions, coverage of public places by CCTV, body scanning at airports, and so on. Many opponents of these measures are likely to object that this will make these democracies less liberal, by infringing the citizens' rights to privacy. We suggest that there is no such moral right, though citizens might have an interest in privacy which currently enjoys the protection of a legal right. It is, however, reasonable to restrict this legal right because, even though the risk of terrorist attacks with weapons of mass destruction might be small, the magnitude of the evil done, were it to occur, could be huge. The multiculturalism typical of modern liberal democracies increases the likelihood that they will be victims of terrorist activity compared to what it would have been had they remained culturally more homogeneous because some of the subcultures they now contain seem unsympathetic to their ideals of liberalism and democracy.

The conception of responsibility as causally-based, which most people tacitly adhere to in everyday life, implies not only that we are more responsible for harms that we cause than for harms that we let happen by our omissions to act, but also that our responsibility for an event is diluted as our causal contribution to it decreases when we act together with other agents to produce it. In Chapter 5, we criticize both of these implications of this conception of responsibility. If we reject this conception, people in rich, developed countries will turn out to be more responsible for the misery occurring in destitute, developing countries than they are spontaneously inclined to think. However, aid to developing countries should not be only of the traditional humanitarian kind—to relieve starvation and diseases and support family planning—it should also include help for these countries to develop in sustainable or environment-friendly ways. Economic development in the affluent countries has been driven by availability of cheap oil, but in order to keep down the emission of greenhouse gases developing countries cannot rely chiefly on fossil fuels to propel their development. And they cannot afford to put in use alternative energy resources without aid from affluent countries. This is one way in which the issue of aid to developing countries is intimately connected with the question at our focus, namely, the question of whether liberal democracies are capable of effectively mitigating anthropogenic or human caused climate change and environmental deterioration. Needless to say, to achieve this aim of preserving the environment and the current climate it is also essential to control population growth in the developing countries.

Chapter 6 presents a well-known cooperation or coordination problem: the tragedy of the commons. In its original terms, this is the problem of whether the herdsmen in a village can trust each other to the extent that it will be rational for each of them to cut down the grazing of their own cattle when this is necessary to prevent over-grazing of their common pastures. It is rational for an individual herdsman to make the sacrifice of cutting down only if he can trust a sufficient number of other herdsmen to do so as well, but it may not be rational for him to have this amount of trust in his fellows. Consequently, most of them might fail to cut down, with the result that they will all starve eventually. We consider the tragedy of the commons because it can serve as a simplified small-scale model of bigger environmental problems. Generally speaking, the larger the number of participants in a cooperative venture, the harder this problem becomes, the more inevitable the tragedy. This is because it is then more difficult for the participants to have concern for and trust in each other. Also, it is more difficult for them to detect defection and free-riding. Furthermore, as the number of participants expands, the damage caused by each individual participant will decrease, until it eventually becomes negligible or imperceptible. Then, according to the conception of responsibility as causally-based, the individuals will not feel any responsibility for the damage done. This undercuts the altruistic or utilitarian reason that the collective could benefit by individual restraint. A sense of justice or fairness—that it would be unfair to free-ride on the reductions of others—could still motivate individual participants to make personal sacrifices, but this feeling is unlikely extended to strangers.

In Chapter 7, we argue that the problem of mitigating anthropogenic climate change and environmental destruction is even harder to solve than these hardest instances of the tragedy of the commons. One reason for this is that, even though there is a consensus among most experts about the fact that the human emission of greenhouse gases causally contributes to global climate change, it is nevertheless possible to entertain doubts about how great this human-induced climate change will be given certain levels of emissions—e.g. what will make the global temperature increase by 2°C— and how harmful such a climate change will be for humans and other organisms. In addition, the bias towards the near future that is a prominent feature of human psychology comes into operation because the graver effects of our emissions of greenhouse gases will occur in the more remote future. In fact, substantial damage to the climate that is avoidable by action today will probably not begin to occur until the end of the present century. Therefore, it will not only leave unaffected those of us who are adults today, but even our children. So, our limited and parochial altruism is a further factor that prevents us from rectifying our excessively consum-erist lifestyle. The limitations of our altruism is pertinent also for the reason that, although it is the affluent countries that are responsible for the greatest emissions, it is in general destitute countries in the South that will suffer most from their harmful effects (though Australia and the southwest of the United States will also have their fair share of droughts). Furthermore, the sacrifices of welfare that affluent people will have to make in order to eliminate a destructive impact upon the climate and environment seem so large that it appears unlikely that they will voluntarily take them on. It would rather have to be forced upon them by legislation, but politicians in democracies are unlikely to propose such legislation, since this will probably cause them to lose elections to other politicians whose policies are more laissez-faire and who are for that reason supported by powerful industrial interests. For all these reasons, the prospect that liberal democracies will be able to deal with climatic and environmental problems seems gloomy.

Chapter 8 suggests that it is easier for authoritarian political systems to implement unpopular policies than it is for democracies. A real-life illustration might be that authoritarian China has enforced a mandatory one-child policy for 30 years, while the more democratic India failed in its attempt to impose a similar kind of policy in the 1970s. So, this capacity to implement unpopular policies sometimes gives authoritarian forms of governments an advantage over democratic governments. However, we mention authoritarianism only to bring out a weakness of democracy, not to suggest that it is a preferable form of government all things considered. As history has shown with frightful clarity, authoritarian regimes can go disastrously wrong in ways that to this day no democracy has done, precisely because of this capacity to implement unpopular policies, which often promote only the interests of the ruling class. In our view, the solution to the mega-problems of today, if there is one, lies not in a shift to an authoritarian type government, but in moral enhancement of the citizens in democracies.

In Chapter 9, we consider the idea that democracy will bring history to an 'end' in the sense that democracy will end social and political development by bringing it to the summit. We do not see why democracy should be thought to put an end to history in this sense even if it is the ideal form of government, since the majority of voters might not realize what is best for them and vote for some less than ideal regime. As things stand today, it seems more likely that democracy will bring history to an end in the more tragic sense of bringing about the downfall of civilization because it is incapable of mitigating human induced climate change and environmental degradation. This undermining of conditions of worthwhile life is bad enough, but there is also an increased risk of wars with weapons of mass destruction over shrinking natural resources to take into account.

Sometimes an appeal is made to the so-called jury theorem to buttress the prospects of democracy reaching the right decisions. Imagine that voters are on average only slightly more likely to get it right than wrong when they face two alternatives, e.g. they are right 51 per cent of the time. Then, if the number of voters is huge, a majority of 51 per cent of the voters is almost certain to get it right. The hitch is that, if the biases we have mentioned—e.g. our parochial altruism and bias towards the near future—are in operation concerning climatic and environmental policies, there is reason to believe that voters are more likely to get it wrong than right, and then it is almost certain that a majority will opt for a mistaken policy! Nor should we take it for granted that the right climatic and environmental policy will always be on the table in democracies; powerful business interests that control a lot of the mass media might block this in a market economy.

In Chapter 10, we contend that a moral enhancement of humankind is necessary for there to be a way out of the present predicament. Modern scientific technology provides us with many means that could cause our downfall. If we are to avoid causing catastrophe by misguided employment of these means, we need to be morally motivated to a higher degree (as well as adequately informed about relevant facts). Our democratic systems need the participation of morally enhanced citizens if they are to issue in a wise and responsible employment of the extraordinary potential of modern technology to do good. We could become morally more motivated, morally enhanced, by a more thoroughgoing application of the traditional methods of moral education. But, as already remarked, these methods appear to have had modest success during the last couple of millennia. So, we suggest that we should explore whether our growing knowledge of biology, especially genetics and neurobiology, could deliver supplementary techniques of moral enhancement, such as pharmaceutical drugs or genetic modifications.

The development and application of such techniques is no doubt a risky course to take—it is after all humans in their current morally inept state that must apply them—but we think that our present situation is so desperate that this is a course of action that must be investigated and, depending upon the outcome of that investigation, perhaps deployed. Since we have radically transformed our social and natural environment by scientific technology, while our moral dispositions have virtually remained unchanged, it seems that we would have to consider applying this technology to our own nature to cope with the external environment that we have created around us.

It might be objected that the discovery or invention of effective biomedical means of moral enhancement is so remote in the future that we shall not have access to them in time to avert the catastrophes that threaten us. We do not dispute that this dystopian prediction might turn out to be correct; the relevant research is in its inception and there is no guarantee that it will deliver sufficiently effective means in time. Our claim is merely that the requisite moral enhancement is theoretically possible—we are not biologically or genetically doomed or determined to cause our own destruction—and that we should do what we can to accomplish it. Since it is easier to harm than to benefit, there could be a turning point at which the growth of human powers of action due to scientific technology becomes for the worse, all things considered, because the moral shortcomings of humankind make the risks of catastrophic misuses of these powers too great. Nonetheless, technology needs to become more efficient in order to provide the steadily growing human population on Earth with a decent standard of living without exhausting the resources of the planet. The alternatives of allowing billions of humans to go on living in misery and running the catastrophic risk of misapplications of a tremendously powerful scientific technology are both extremely unappealing.

The risks of misapplying scientific technology are serious because human moral psychology is adapted to life in the very different conditions of small communities with simple technology in which humans have lived during most of their history. Good moral motives were often enough overruled in those small communities with simple technology, but now their failure to guide us could have much more disastrous consequences. We believe that a turning point at which technological and scientific progress changed from being to the overall advantage to being to the overall disadvantage of humanity was passed when, in the middle of the last century, humans acquired the means of forever destroying life on Earth. However, we still need further scientific progress to master the problem that we face today—but this must go with a morally much wiser use of the fruits of this progress than we have shown in the past. It *is* possible for humankind to improve morally to the extent that the overwhelming powers of action that modern scientific technology affords will be used for the better, all things considered. The very progress of science and technology increases this possibility by promising to supply new instruments of moral enhancement, which could be applied alongside traditional moral education.

We highlight biomedical means of moral enhancement, not because we believe that they will necessarily be more effective than traditional means of moral enhancement, or than various kinds of social reform which abolish familial, economical, educational, etc. conditions that stunt the development of people, but because many people reject them out of hand for untenable reasons. We give a couple of examples of how moral behaviour can be influenced by biomedical means in order to demonstrate that moral bioenhancement is not just a theoretical possibility, but has been practised. But this line of research is still in its infancy, so it has as yet produced no convincing results, and perhaps it will not do so in time even if diligently pursued. Consequently, it is also too early in the day to tell what a programme of more extensive moral bioenhancement could look like and how it could be fitted in with more thoroughgoing traditional moral education and with various possible reforms of laws and other social institutions. Our ambition is merely to put some proposals on the agenda, not to launch any definitive and detailed solution to the mega-problems that we discuss. Perhaps there is no realistic solution to all of them. Perhaps, sadly, human beings will waste most of the huge potential to do good that modern scientific technology offers them.

2

Human Nature and Common-Sense Morality

In this chapter, we attempt to draw a map of common-sense morality and some related psychological dispositions. By 'common-sense morality' we mean a set of moral attitudes that is a common denominator of the diversely specified moralities of human societies over the world. We take it that the explanation of why there is a set of moral attitudes that is a common feature of culturally diverse moralities is that it has its origin in our evolutionary history. However, it should not be thought that we regard common-sense morality to be sacrosanct and beyond criticism. Quite the contrary, we believe that it is in need of thorough revision. Moreover, we believe that its deficiencies, and the deficiencies of the related psychological dispositions, make us ill-equipped to cope with the moral problems generated by the advanced scientific technology, over-population, and the globalization of the modern world.

As human beings compete with each other over the scarce resources of nature, they are prone to cause harm to one another. Now it is a fact of life that it is in general easier for humans to cause each other harm than to benefit each other. To give an everyday illustration: most of the readers of this book probably have access to a car and live in densely populated areas. Whenever you drive, you could easily kill a number of people, by ploughing into a crowd. But, we dare say, very few of you have the opportunity every day to save the lives of an equal number. Indeed, most of you have probably never had that opportunity, since this kind of situation obtains only when, first, a large number of lives is threatened, and, secondly, you are also in a position to eliminate that threat. So, our claim is not that people are never capable of saving as many individuals as would die if a threat were not successfully foiled. Rather, we are claiming that in order to save a number of lives, people have to find themselves in situations in which these lives are under a threat that they could avert. This is a comparatively rare event beyond their control. By contrast, they frequently have the opportunity to kill many.

It might be objected that people in affluent countries have the opportunity of saving many lives in developing countries by donating relatively small sums of money to the most cost-effective aid agencies. True, but, again, this is because we happen to find ourselves in special circumstances, which are conducive to our providing great benefits, namely a huge global inequality in which we are vastly better off than many of those who need our help. Moreover, we could accomplish these greatly beneficial deeds only because there are already in place, due to the work of many good-natured people, highly cost-effective aid agencies. Therefore, we cannot justifiably claim anything approaching the whole credit for the lives saved by our donations. Imagine how many we could have killed if there were equally cost-effective 'harm' agencies which offered cheap ways of killing when, as we have seen, most of us could single-handedly and in the everyday run of things kill a two-digit number of people.[1]

We could distinguish between two related aspects of the greater easiness or power to cause harm. First, the *magnitude* of the harm caused can be greater than the magnitude of the benefits provided: for instance, we can generally kill more individuals than we can save the lives of, wound more than we could heal the wounds of, cause pain which is more intense than the pleasure that we can cause. The driving example was meant to illustrate this aspect. Secondly, there are many more *ways or means* of causing harm of a given magnitude than there are ways of benefiting to the same degree. This is because there are more ways of disturbing a well-functioning system, like a biological organism, or the interaction of organisms like an ecosystem, than of improving it to the same extent. Thus, arbitrary interferences with well-functioning systems are much more likely to damage them than to improve them. Furthermore, their order or degree of organization tends to decrease in the course of time because most changes in them will damage them. This is a part of what is known as entropy. If we remove *any* of the countless conditions, which are necessary to maintain the functioning of an integrated system, we shall interrupt its function, but in order to improve its function, we have to discover a

---

[1] For further discussion of this point, see our reply (Persson and Savulescu, 2011) to John Harris, 2011.

condition which fits in so well with all these conditions that the function is enhanced. Such conditions are likely to be far fewer, so this task is much harder.

This is the main reason why it is in general easier to kill than to save life. There are innumerable conditions which are necessary for an organism to continue to be alive. Thus, we could kill it by finding out which of these conditions is easiest for us to remove, and remove it. As there are many ways of killing an organism, there is likely to be some within our reach. By contrast, to save its life we have no choice but to restore something like the particular condition removed, however difficult that may be.

But imagine that, contrary to what we have argued, it would be as easy to save life as to kill; then it would still not follow that, if we were to save a life, we could claim credit for as much benefits as we would be guilty of harm if we were to end it. This is again because there are countless conditions necessary for an organism to remain alive. If we remove any of these conditions, we are guilty of ending this life forever. But if we prevent the removal of such a condition, we cannot claim the whole credit for the continuation of this life, since there are other conditions necessary for keeping this life going on. So, our lifesaving action is necessary but not by itself sufficient to sustain the life, while our act of killing is by itself sufficient to end it.

Suppose now that life is good for the organism as long as it naturally lasts. If we remove any of the conditions which are requisite to sustain this life, we kill the organism. We thereby deprive it of all the future good that its life would have contained had it not ended prematurely. Thus, by removing any of those conditions, we are guilty of causing it a harm, which equals the loss of the goodness of which it is deprived. But if we had instead saved the organism from death at the same time, we cannot claim credit for all the good that the future has in store for it, since this saving is only one of the indefinitely many conditions necessary for it to lead this future good life. Consequently, the benefit we would bestow upon an individual by saving its life at a time would be less than the harm we would do it were we to kill it at the same time, for our saving its life is not sufficient for it to receive the future good life, whereas the killing is sufficient to deprive it of it. Therefore, even if it had been as easy to save life as to kill—which we have argued that it is not—it would not be true that our capacity to benefit would be as great as our capacity to harm by these means.

In this argument we have been assuming that life is worthwhile, at least better than non-existence. However, if Arthur Schopenhauer and other pessimists, like David Benatar (2006), are right that life is always worse than non-existence, then the opposite would hold: by killing somebody, we would benefit them much more than we would harm them were we instead to save their life. We shall however proceed on the assumption that life, or at least human life, is normally better than non-existence, since we believe that this is the view that most of us would take. (But even if human life is normally better than non-existence, it should not be forgotten that it is sometimes worse than death. This is what makes euthanasia morally justified at times.)

Now, our claim is strictly about benefiting and harming. It concerns saving life and killing, curing and wounding, etc., only derivatively, i.e. in so far as they are means of benefiting and harming. However, there is a danger in talking about benefiting and harming because these concepts are more abstract. One might be misled into thinking that benefiting could consist in simply omitting to harm. If this were so, it would not be easier to harm than to benefit, since it is easier to omit harming than to harm, e.g. easier to omit killing than to kill. But this view of benefiting is mistaken: it takes an *action* to benefit, e.g. an action of lifesaving, just as it takes an action to harm. If omitting to harm were benefiting, then the act-omission doctrine—which, as will emerge below, implies that harming is morally worse than omitting to benefit—would be *self-contradictory* rather than merely morally mistaken. For this doctrine would then imply that harming could be worse than omitting to omit harming, i.e. that it could be worse than harming, which is obviously a contradiction. We do reject the act-omission doctrine, but it would be question-begging to base this rejection upon a definition which makes the doctrine self-contradictory. Benefiting (harming) individuals is acting so that they become better (worse) off than they would be in the absence of this action. If there was no such a notion of benefiting (and of harming), but benefiting was nothing other than not harming or omitting to harm, we would be caught in a very tight circle when defining the notions of benefiting and harming. We believe that, contrary to the act-omission doctrine, failing to benefit may be as morally wrong or bad as harming, but this does not mean that they are the same.

The fact that we are more exposed to grave threats of harm than to great expectations of benefits explains, we hypothesize, why we exhibit what Daniel Kahneman and Amos Tversky call *loss aversion*, i.e. that for us 'losses loom larger than gains' (2000: 46). A simple illustration of loss aversion is that people in general demand a much higher price to sell an item that they own than they offer to buy the same kind of item. Similarly, it has been observed that people are reluctant to take a bet in which there is a 50 per cent probability that they will lose 100 dollars alongside a 50 per cent probability that they will win, say, 125 dollars. The win has to be close to 200 dollars in order for people to be willing to take the bet, i.e. it takes almost a doubling of the win to outweigh the risk of losing the 100 dollars.[2]

In contrast, most of us happily accept, as Kahneman and Tversky point out, a very high risk, amounting to virtual certainty, of a small loss in order to obtain a vanishingly small chance of a very great gain. This is something that we often do when we buy a lottery ticket, or gamble. Hence, loss aversion can be offset by the likelihood of obtaining a very much bigger gain, even if the likelihood of getting it is exceedingly small. We are thus subject to what could be called a *big gain attraction*. This tendency has a negative counterpart, a version of simple loss aversion, *big loss aversion,* or more generally, a *disproportionately* strong aversion to great harm, i.e. an aversion that is stronger than the expected disvalue of the harm, which is obtained by multiplying the actual disvalue of the harm with the probability of it. As the magnitude of a loss increases, our aversion to that increasing loss could grow disproportionately.

We believe that part of the explanation of big gain attraction and big loss aversion is that our conative–affective reactions are not finely attuned to small differences in probability, except when this amounts to a change to certainty or impossibility. Thus, an increase in the probability of a big loss, or other great harm, from 0.75 to 0.80 does not noticeably affect our emotion of fear, while an increase from 0.95 to 1 could change our fear to horror.[3] So, a loss or harm, which is big enough to stir up our fear, will do

---

[2] Loss aversion is sometimes not distinguished from a form of psychological inertia that has been called 'the status quo bias': a failure to make changes with respect to present circumstances, though there is a perceived reason to do so, e.g. the failure to sign a donor card (consequently, the number of potential donors in an 'opt-out' system will be considerably higher than in an 'opt-in' system). The cause of our failure to act in such situations is however not aversion to any risk of loss, but that it takes some effort to act, and we do not get around to summoning up enough energy to make this effort because we are preoccupied with more pressing matters. So we procrastinate.

[3] This deficient sensitivity to probabilities is akin to, but not the same as, the notion of a diminishing sensitivity to probabilities the greater their distance from impossibility and

so to the same degree, irrespective of whether the risk of it is, say, 0.05 or 0.1; similarly, for a gain or benefit that is big enough to stir up our hopes or wishes. Thus, a great gain of which there is only miniscule probability, like winning the lottery, could stir up our feelings more than a small loss which is certain, like paying the price of the lottery ticket.

To give a simple example of the disproportionately strong aversion to great harm, suppose that we could assign numerical values to units of well-being or welfare, i.e. what is intrinsically good or bad for us, like pleasure and pain, and that we could assign numerical values to the relevant probabilities.[4] Consider now a choice between a 99 per cent probability of suffering a few minutes of a very mild, barely noticeable pain of -2 units, and a 1 per cent probability of suffering an equally long, quite severe pain which is 50 times as strong, -100. Standard decision theory would declare it rational to choose the latter, since the expected disvalue of former alternative is almost twice as great. Nonetheless, most of us will probably regard it as reasonable to opt for the former alternative. The explanation is, we surmise, that our emotional reaction is geared more to the great difference in intensity between these pains than to smaller differences in probability: our fear of the greater pain is as strong as it would be if the probability had been, say, 5 per cent.

Turn now to a case which involves a possible big loss of benefits. Consider whether it is worth exposing yourself to a small risk of 1 per cent, say, of losing large benefits, of 100 units, that you possess in order to have a 99 per cent chance of gaining an extra 2 units. An example could be an operation that will almost certainly correct a small defect of yours, e.g. in your visual or motor ability, but which could conceivably go seriously wrong, though this is most unlikely, and make you blind or paralysed. The expected value of the possible improvement is nearly twice the expected disvalue of the possible loss. So, according to standard decision theory it would be rational to undergo the operation. But again it would strike

---

certainty which, alongside loss aversion, figures in Kahneman and Tversky's alternative to expected utility theory, 'prospect theory' (2000: 50). As opposed to them, we do not claim e.g. that an increase in probability from 0.85 to 0.90 will have a greater impact upon our conative-affective state than an increase from 0.55 to 0.60.

[4] We give reasons for doubting the former supposition in Ch. 4. As regards assignments of numerical values to probabilities, they are straightforward in cases in which they are based on the frequencies of outcomes, e.g. the number of times that coins flipped come up with heads. They are considerably more controversial in other cases, e.g. the probability that Shakespeare wrote all the plays commonly attributed to him.

many of us as almost insane to run even such a small risk as one in a hundred of being blind or paralysed in order to gain an increase of well-being which is relatively insignificant. We are then in the grip of big loss aversion, i.e. loss aversion which is amplified by a disproportionately strong worry about greater harm.

Furthermore, our greater proneness to being harmed makes it comprehensible that the negative emotion of fear is more widespread and could be considerably more intense than its positive counterpart of hope or longing: as a rule, there is more in the world for us to shrink back from than to be drawn towards. Fear could be intensified into terror and horror, but there is no counterpart to this intensification in the case of hope or longing. Likewise, in a world in which most of the time we risk losing more than we could reasonably hope to gain, and in which we compete with each other over scarce resources, it has survival value that the negative reaction of anger be more widespread and stronger than its positive counterpart of gratitude, since it will be more important to scare off attackers than to return favours done by do-gooders. Hence, it is not surprising that anger could increase to fury and rage, but that there is nothing corresponding to this intensity in the case of gratitude. For a similar reason, the signal of something's going wrong in your body, that is, physical pain, can be more intense and bring more suffering than the signal of something's going well—pleasure—can bring enjoyment.

It might then be wondered why we are not constantly in the grip of fear due to big loss aversion, since we are constantly exposed to some risk of suffering big losses, e.g. we could die or suffer serious injury at any moment. The answer probably lies in what has been called *the availability bias* (e.g. by Sunstein, 2007: 6, following Kahneman and Tversky): we are fixated on the possible occurrence of events of which we have readily available images, largely as a result of recently having experienced events of these kinds. We spontaneously imagine that what has not been observed, e.g. the future, will resemble that which has been observed in the past.[5] Now our emotions seem geared to how vividly we imagine significantly positive or negative events rather than to how probable we estimate them to be. To take an everyday example, you might cycle to work every day in

---

[5] This mechanism of association figures prominently in David Hume's discussion of causation (1739–40/1978: I. iii). In Persson, 2005: 104, it is called the mechanism of spontaneous induction.

heavy traffic, without feeling any fear of being the victim of a nasty accident, though you know that there is a non-negligible probability that you might be. But if you do have a nasty accident, or are on the verge of having one, this might make you so terrified of cycling in the traffic that you are unable to do so for quite some time. It is not that the detailed memory of the recent accident makes your estimate of the probability of another, similar accident rise steeply; instead, it makes you imagine more vividly what it is like to have such an accident. In the course of time, the intensity of this memory usually fades, and with it the intensity of images of possible accidents in the future, so eventually your fear might subside, and you might be able to resume your cycling.[6] Accordingly, the reason why the big loss aversion does not keep us in a constant state of fear, though we constantly face risks of big losses, is that we do not vividly imagine ourselves experiencing these losses, since we are accustomed to escaping them. That is to say, the availability bias often counteracts big loss aversion.

Owing to the relative easiness of causing harm, common-sense morality, which has presumably evolved to enable (smaller) groups of around 100 humans to live together in ways that promote the survival and reproduction of the group overall, places more stress on not causing harm than on doing good. This stress on not harming takes, we propose, the form of a *doctrine of negative rights*, according to which we have rights against others that they do *not* interfere with the use that we could make of ourselves and the property that we have acquired by our own efforts. The evolutionary origin of such rights does not appear hard to understand, since they could be construed as derivative from behavioural traits like the special ferocity with which non-human animals defend themselves, their turf, food, and so on. This ferocity provides a reason for others to leave these items alone—a reason which is expressed by the notion of a right. The 'other side' of these rights is corresponding negative duties or obligations of others to not interfere with us and our property. By contrast, other persons do not have any positive duties or obligations to help us maintain our life and property; they have only weaker moral reasons of beneficence to provide such aid.

A common-sense morality of this asymmetrical sort is to be expected in a world in which beings, when they have matured, are normally fit to

---

[6] This is a phenomenon noticed already by Hume, 1739–40/1978: I. iii.13.

survive by their own means, to find the food, shelter, and other things that they need. A world inhabited by beings who were constantly dependent upon aid from other beings to the same extent as they were when they grew up would not be functional; too much aid from others would be needed for it to go around. It is much easier to satisfy needs to be spared violent assaults because this is accomplished simply by not acting—i.e. by omissions—but norms to this effect would nevertheless contribute significantly to peaceful coexistence.

It important to recognize, however, that when we are here discussing the content of what we take to be common sense or folk morality, the kind of morality that has naturally evolved in human communities, we are not assuming that this morality is true or justified. Consequently, we are not exposing ourselves to what G. E. Moore (1903: 10) famously called the *naturalistic fallacy* of attempting to deduce norms from natural facts. The point is not that we are assuming that such a deduction is fallacious; it is merely that we are not committed to any such deduction, so it is irrelevant whether or not it is valid.

John Locke has given classical expression to the kind of doctrine of rights sketched here:

every man has a property in his own person. This nobody has any right to but himself. The labour of his body and the work of his hands, we may say, are properly his. Whatsoever, then, he removes out of the state that Nature hath provided and left it in, he hath mixed his labour with it, and joined to it something that is his own, and thereby makes it his property (1690/1990: II. v. 27).

It is well known, even by right theorists like Robert Nozick (1974: 174–5; see also Waldron, 1988: chs. 6 and 7), that this attempt to ground rights to things that nature provides turns out to be deeply problematic. (This is compatible with it being a ground that we could spontaneously accept in everyday life because seeing that it is problematic takes reflection.) To begin with, the notion of 'mixing one's labour' with something is perplexing: we can mix other things by our labour, but we cannot mix our labour with anything. Let us take it that what is at issue is simply some act of appropriating or acquiring something 'out of the state that Nature hath provided and left it in', i.e. appropriating it before anyone else does.

A fundamental difficulty then concerns how one's having the factual relation of appropriation to something, X, could have a normative significance to the effect of imposing a *duty* upon others, a duty to the effect that they do not help themselves to X even if they need it more. It is not mysterious that we could be spontaneously inclined to *believe* that something like this is true. This belief could have a useful peace-preserving function in a community, by saving its members many conflicts or disputes over material possessions; they would agree that whoever gets to it first should have it. What is mysterious is how this belief could be *true*: how the natural fact that one is first to lay one's hands upon some natural resource could place others under an obligation (or an especially strong reason) to leave one in possession or use of the resource, and make their attempted acquisition of it unjust, even if they are much greater need of it. This again raises the issue of the naturalistic fallacy.

It would not have been mysterious how this natural relation could have had such a normative significance if people beforehand had voluntarily agreed to take it to impose duties upon them. This is because it would then be these people who would impose duties upon themselves by their agreement, like people agreeing to abide by the rules of some game. However, such an antecedent agreement is not in operation here. Instead, we face a situation in which the fact that someone else has been the first one to acquire something, perhaps merely by being lucky enough to find it before anyone else on a stroll in the countryside, could impose on you a duty to let the putative right holder keep it, or make it unjust that you acquire (some of) it, though you need it more. This is hard to make credible.

Due to this difficulty, and some others to be delineated soon, we think that it is better to try to make do without any appeal to Lockean rights. We shall instead appeal to *benefits* and *harms*, or things that are intrinsically good or bad for us. This shift lies close at hand because there is a conceptual connection between rights, on the one hand, and benefits and harms, on the other. A necessary condition for our having a right to X is that X is something that we could put to a use that is in itself good for us, or that benefits us. We are not described as having rights to things that are bad for us, or that we would like to be rid of, like the excrement or garbage we produce. The same goes for things that are a matter of indifference for us. The things to which we are thought to have rights cannot meaningfully be such that we are at all times willing to waive our rights to them; the right to such things would be pointless. Nonetheless, the things to which we are held to have rights are not identical to anything that is in itself good for us. They are rather *resources* which could *generate* something that is of value for us if we put them to use, e.g. it is the pleasure or desire-fulfilment, which we derive from eating the food, to which we have a right that is a benefit, or something that is intrinsically good for us.

For the purpose of some of the problems discussed in this work, the feasibility of this shift from moral rights to benefits is important. This is because a morality of rights makes it hard to explain how it could be morally relevant to take into consideration merely possible individuals; individuals who would exist were we to act differently, e.g. those different individuals who would exist if we implemented different, more sustainable environmental policies. Merely possible individuals surely do not possess any rights that could be violated. By contrast, it makes more sense to claim (although it is controversial whether it is in the end justifiable) that we could benefit and harm possible individuals, by giving or denying them worthwhile lives.[7] It should, however, be mentioned that rights are designed to provide stronger moral reasons—as they put others under duties or obligations—than do the interests that they protect. Therefore, the abandonment of rights will mean that in conflicts the no longer right-protected interests of a single individual could more easily be outweighed by the weaker interests of many other individuals and, so, that it could be morally justifiable to sacrifice one individual for the smaller good of each of a greater number of individuals.

Another feature of common-sense morality is a *conception of responsibility as causally-based*, according to which we are more responsible for things, e.g. violations of rights, which we commit, or cause, than for things that we let happen by our omissions to prevent them. The idea is not that we have *no* responsibility for what we let happen through our omissions, e.g. that a person who stands on the shore and lets someone drown is as innocent with respect to this death as another person who is not even in the vicinity. Rather, we have *some* responsibility, but it is so weak that, for instance, it is rarely recognized by the law.[8] A conception of responsibility

---

[7] In other words, it becomes possible to solve what Parfit calls *the non-identity problem* (1984: ch. 16; Persson, 2009), but of course this kind of solution brings along other consequences, which many find counterintuitive, e.g. that there could be moral reason to bring happy individuals into existence for their own sakes. These are, however, problems that we will not discuss here.

[8] More precisely, responsibility is weaker unless we have a special duty or obligation to save life, as e.g. a lifeguard has. It could be a criminal offence to omit discharging a special duty. Special duties or obligations are discussed below.

that is based upon what is physically caused has the advantage—crucial in our prehistory—of being more straightforwardly applicable to individuals than a conception of responsibility that refers to their mental states, such as the intentions and beliefs which explain their actions. The reason for this is that one cannot observe the mental states of other agents than oneself, while what these agents cause with their bodily actions obviously can be.

We do not take ourselves to cause what we let happen by our omissions to act. Consider a simple omission, such as omitting to move your hand, and letting it remain where it is, resting on a horizontal plane (and thereby letting other things happen as a consequence). You decide for some reason not to move your hand and, as a result, you do not move it. The result, your not moving your hand, is the same as it could be if you had made no decision at all, but had, say, lost consciousness. But there is a difference: when you do not move your hand because you decide not to move it, the position of your hand is in accordance with your decision, while of course this cannot be the case in the second situation in which you make no decision. This difference is an essential part of what we mean by saying that you are *omitting* to move your hand, or *letting* it remain where it is, in the first situation, but not in the second. The occurrence of your decision is logically necessary for your not moving your hand to be describable as omitting to move it (or as refraining from moving it), and letting it be unmoved. But it is not *causally* necessary for your not moving hand, since if we abstract your decision, but leave other simultaneous conditions intact—in particular, do not add conditions such as a decision to move your hand—your not moving your hand would still have resulted.

Certainly, something can be a cause without being causally necessary. This happens when there is overdetermination, but it would be implausible to claim that whenever you omit moving your hand, there is another cause of its not moving, alongside your decision not to move it—a cause that could be present when your decision is not. It is more reasonable to think there is then simply an *absence* of other events, which would have caused it to move. So, the reasonable conclusion is that your decision not to move your hand (and its neural correlate) is not a cause of your hand's not moving. This is not a surprising conclusion: it is as little a surprise that a decision not to cause something, e.g. your hand to move, does not cause this, as that a decision to cause something, e.g. your hand to move, causes this. And if in a situation in which you decide whether or not to move your hand, there is no independent cause of its moving, your decision not to cause it to move will issue in it not moving simply because there is no cause of its moving.

Nonetheless, it is surely true that you did not move your hand *because* you decided not to. What is the force of this explanation if your decision is not a cause? A plausible idea is that citing this decision explains your hand's not moving by excluding causes of it moving, i.e. by excluding that you decided to move your hand in this way or that, which (or the neural correlate of which) would have caused your hand to move in this way or that. When it has been established that there was nothing that would cause your hand to move at the relevant time, there is nothing more that needs to be done to explain why it did not move at the time. To conclude, when we omit acting, and thereby let something be the case, we do not cause anything. Therefore, according the conception of responsibility as causally-based, we are less responsible for things we let happen, though there might still be a basis for assigning *some* responsibility for them, since we could have prevented them.

It is worth noting that this conception of responsibility goes beyond the doctrine of rights in that it implies that we are more responsible for rights-violations that we commit than for rights-violations that we let others commit. It is logically possible to have a theory of rights, according to which it is as wrong to let someone else violate a right as it is to violate it oneself—for instance, to let another responsible agent kill as to kill with one's own hands. By incorporating a conception of responsibility as causally-based, common-sense morality rules out a theory of rights of this sort. In this way, a causal conception of responsibility makes morality practicable, i.e. our moral duties or obligations become more easily dischargeable and, for that reason, can be more stringent.

Causally-based responsibility is proportionally diluted when we cause things together with other agents, e.g. when we together destroy a lawn by each of us walking across it from time to time, since our own causal contribution to the deterioration of the lawn then decreases compared to what it would have been had we destroyed the lawn on our own. We shall have occasion to return to this phenomenon since, as already remarked, we live and act in vastly populous societies, and it is highly relevant to our topic of anthropogenic climate change and environmental degradation.

We are now in a position to spell out a further theoretical difficulty with the common-sense concept of a (property) right to something. Suppose that we agree that you have a right to X because you have been the first to have appropriated it. Even so, you will not have that relation of appropriation to every proper part of X; for instance, you will not have been the first one to have appropriated all of the micro particles composing X. They are not even the sort of thing that you could appropriate or acquire. On the account given of the ground for these rights, you would therefore not have any rights to these parts of X. But it is paradoxical to maintain that you could have a right to X, although it could be divided into parts to which you do not have any right, for then you could be deprived of X without your rights being violated. This could happen by your being deprived of all the parts of X to which you have no right, one by one.[9]

Imagine that innumerable agents act in concert to remove all the micro particles of which X is composed, each agent snatching only a single one of these particles. (X could be anything material to which you are held to have a right, either your own body or something external to it.) Then, according to the conception of responsibility as causally-based, none of these agents will be responsible for a violation of your rights since, as just remarked, you do not have any right to the individual particles composing X. Nor will anyone of these agents be responsible for causing you any harm, for presumably the removal of a single particle makes no perceptible difference for you. Yet the upshot of this collective act would be the same as if one agent had deprived you of the whole of X at one go and, by hypothesis, had violated your right. This shows that moral rights do not under all circumstances provide effective protection, and that the protection they offer could in principle be circumvented.

Despite these difficulties, let us however continue to spell out the content of the commonsensical theory of rights. Suppose that you endanger the life of someone, by pushing her into a stream. Then, by performing this act of pushing, for which you are responsible according to the causally-based conception of responsibility, you incur a *special* duty or obligation to save that individual's life—if so, this individual has a corresponding *special* right against you, to have her life saved by you. This right is special because it holds only against *you*, as opposed to the rights to life, limb, and property mentioned above which are *general* because they hold against *everybody* who is capable of recognizing rights:

---

[9] For further elaboration of this argument, see Persson, 1994.

everybody should refrain from interfering with the life, etc. of others.[10] As the example of the right to be saved by you shows, special rights can be positive, in contrast to general rights, which we have seen to be negative.

When human beings acquired the use of language, they could employ their recognition that they are instinctively disposed to regard themselves as being able to place themselves under special obligations by their actions as a model for the speech act of *promising*. The function of issuing of a promise to do something, for instance, to give some aid, is precisely to shoulder an obligation towards the promisee to perform that act. By means of speech acts such as promising, we not only extend the range of special obligations that we could undertake beyond those most obviously called for by our present conduct, we could also make their content more precise, since we can promise not only to perform very specific actions, but also, e.g. to perform them at specific times, even in the remote future. Analogously, we could *waive* or *transfer* rights that we have by performing speech acts, say, by giving our (informed and voluntary) consent to a physician's treating us in some way; we give her permission to treat us in some way that she would not be permitted to treat us without our consent.

The doctrine of negative rights and the conception of responsibility as causally-based apparently underlies the so-called *act-omission doctrine*, the doctrine that it is more difficult morally to justify causing certain kinds of harm, e.g. death, than it is morally to justify letting these kinds of harm to occur, e.g. letting somebody die or be killed, by omissions to act.[11] According to such a construal of the act-omission doctrine, the relevant harms will be ones that involve an infringement of some right, e.g. the right to life. Thus, when an act or an omission is not relevant to some right, there is no moral difference between acts and omissions. It is consequently no more difficult morally to justify harming someone by seeing to it that he does not get the first prize in a contest by fairly beating him than it is to let him be fairly beaten by somebody else. The reason is

---

[10] The distinction between general and special rights was introduced by Hart, 1955.

[11] The act-omission doctrine is sometimes called the doctrine of doing and allowing. Some authors seem to think that these doctrines are different because they count as instances of allowing something to happen, or letting it happen, some cases in which you *act*, so that, for instance, when you turn off life-sustaining aid, you could be said to let the patient die. But in our view these are not pure cases of letting something happen; they are cases of acting *and then* letting something happen by omitting some other actions, e.g. starting the life-sustaining aid again. For our conception of letting something happen which implies that this occurs by omitting to act, see Persson and Savulescu, 2005: 12–3, and Persson, 2007a: 19–20.

that no contestant has a right to win the prize, though they do have rights not to be killed, injured or robbed.[12] (As already indicated, we could however imagine an account of rights, according to which it is equally hard to justify letting a right be violated as violating it oneself. The fact that this is not so according to the rights theory endorsed by common sense is explained by the fact that it also incorporates a causally-based conception of responsibility, making us more responsible for what we do than for what we let happen.[13])

We will now turn to consider other relevant features of our moral psychology. Since the tools and other means at our disposal in the long pre-scientific period of our history enabled us to affect only our immediate environment in the imminent future, and imminent dangers tended to be most urgent to deal with in order to survive and reproduce, we have a *bias towards the near future*. It is this bias which manifests itself when we are relieved if something unpleasant due to happen to us in the near future is postponed, and disappointed if something pleasant in store for us in the near future is postponed, whereas the same postponement of unpleasant and pleasant in the more distant future would leave us unaffected.

There is a discounting of future events which is rational because it is as a rule true that, when an event is in the more remote future, it is less probable than what is closer to the present, and the lower probability of an event's occurring makes it rational to be proportionally less concerned about it (this is the notion of expected utility in standard decision theory). But it would be a mistake to think that the bias towards the near future consists in being less concerned about an event in store for us in the more remote future because it is estimated to be less probable. For we could be greatly relieved when an unpleasant event, such as a painful piece of surgery, is postponed for just a day, even though we take this delay to make it only marginally less probable. To the extent that our lesser concern for what is more distant in the future is out of proportion to its being estimated to be less probable, it is arguably not rational. The bias

---

[12] More precisely, contestants do not have a right to the prize in the sense in which a right corresponds to a duty of others to let them win the prize. This has been called a *claim* right as opposed to a *liberty* right, which is merely the absence of an obligation; for instance, to say that all competitors have a right to win the prize in the liberty sense is to say that they are not under any obligation to abstain from winning it. In this book we generally reserve the term 'right' for the stronger sense of a claim right, and talk of liberty in the latter case.

[13] For further discussion of these matters, see Persson, 2007a.

towards the near future appears to be the explanation of why we exhibit weakness of will by choosing, against our better judgement, to have a smaller good straightaway rather than to wait some extra hours for a much greater good. This behaviour seems clearly irrational, and we usually regret it with the benefit of hindsight.[14]

Nevertheless, the fact that what is more distant in the future relative to the present time is as a rule less probable and, thus, less urgent from the point of view of survival and reproduction, could be the evolutionary explanation of why we are endowed with the bias towards the near future. This bias has survival value for beings who do not have the capacity to make reliable estimates of probability relating to future events, which was surely true of humans during most of their history when their knowledge of the workings of the world was very limited. What this remark brings out is that we must be careful to distinguish between what is the evolutionary explanation or reason of why we have a certain trait and what is *our* reason or motive when we act and react in accordance with this trait (cf. Joyce, 2006: 17–8). When we are subject to the bias towards the near future, our reason for being less concerned about what is more distant in time is simply that it is more distant, not that it is less probable. This is, however, compatible with the explanation or reason of why we are equipped with this bias, being that what is more distant in time is generally less probable and, thus, of less urgency to our weal and woe. To bring home the distinction made, a simpler illustration of it may be helpful: our reason for wanting to have sex is often that we think it will give us pleasure, but the evolutionary explanation of why we have this reason which makes us want sex presumably has to do with the propagation of our genes.

It might be asked whether we are also biased towards what is near to us in *space*. Our view is that there is no spatial bias which is parallel to the bias towards the near future. The bias towards the near future is most pronounced as regards to things that could happen to *ourselves* in the near and remote future—it is an *egocentric* bias. By contrast, we are surely not biased towards what could be happening to us at places that are close to our present place, as opposed to places that are more remote from it. We would care as much about something happening to us were we at some

---

[14] For further discussion of the bias towards the near future, see Parfit, 1984: pt. II, and Persson, 2005: ch. 14. It has been experimentally studied e.g. by Walter Mischel, 1974.

place remote from our present place as about it happening to us were we close to our present place. If you have some bodily condition, which regularly occasions you pain, you spontaneously care about whether this will happen to you in the near or distant future, but you would not care about whether it will happen to you when you are at a place which is near to or distant from your present place. So, it is implausible to think that we are equipped with an egocentric bias towards what is spatially near, as we are equipped with an egocentric bias towards what is temporally near.

As will soon surface, we are capable of having strong concern not only for our own welfare, but also for the welfare of other beings with whom we are personally acquainted. We do not exhibit a spatial bias with respect to such acquaintances just as we do not do with respect to ourselves. Should your sympathetic concern be aroused by a loved one who is suffering, your concern is not dampened if you learn that they are far away rather than close by. However, it is true that, other things being equal, you would spontaneously care more about there being a *stranger* now starving in your cellar than about there being a stranger now starving in Africa. This would be so even if you knew that you are as incapable of doing anything about the suffering in the former as in the latter case because you are prevented from entering your cellar. You would still be inclined to feel a stronger regret that you could not do anything about the situation in the former case. That is to say, with respect to other individuals for whom your sympathetic concern has not already been aroused, considerations of spatial distance relative to you seem to affect the degree to which your concern is aroused: the closer their position is to yours, the stronger your concern. But such spatial considerations do not appear to affect the degree of your concern once it has been aroused.

The explanation of why spatial closeness contributes to arousal might be that when we are told that something is occurring close by, we are prone to think more—and consequently to feel more—about it, since we are accustomed to it being the case that when something occurs nearby, we can do something about it and, so, need to think about what to do. This habit is apparently so inveterate that it is not defeated by a reflective conviction that in particular cases we are powerless to rectify something that occurs close by, as we imagined in the case of the stranger starving in your cellar. In contrast, it is hard to see why evolution should have provided us with a disposition which could tempt us to smother our already aroused sympathetic concern for sufferers by simply increasing our distance to them, so to speak fleeing from the inclination to help them. Hence, we are endowed with a spatial bias which is partially, but only partially, analogous to the bias towards the near future. Its being only partially analogous makes it of less importance than our temporal bias to the near, since it does not tempt us to irrationally discount the significance of anyone's well-being in a way that would incline us to increase our distance to sufferers at the expense of making their suffering worse. By contrast, our temporal bias to the near future causes us to postpone irrationally our own suffering at the expense of making it worse.[15]

Apart from biased considerations of time and space, the sheer *number* of subjects to whom we have to respond can present another obstacle to our adoption of a proper moral response. While many of us are capable of vividly imagining the suffering of a single subject before our eyes and, consequently, of feeling strong compassion for this subject, we are unable to imagine vividly the suffering of, say, ten subjects even if they be in sight—indeed, we could barely vividly imagine the suffering of more than one subject. Nor could we feel a compassion which is ten times as strong as the compassion we could feel for a single sufferer. Rather, the degree of our felt compassion is likely to remain more or less constant when we switch from reflecting upon the suffering of a single subject to the suffering of ten subjects. Yet the cost of relieving the suffering of ten subjects may well be ten times as high as the cost of relieving the suffering of one subject. Therefore, it is not surprising that, as the number of subjects in need of aid increases, the amount of aid that we are willing to give to each subject decreases. This is sometimes called *scope insensitivity* (or scope neglect),[16] though *number insensitivity or numbness* would seem to be more apt names.

As already observed, the bias towards the near future is an egocentric bias: it is manifested in the concern that we have for our own good in the near future. In the history of philosophy many thinkers have been *psychological egoists*, that is, they have thought that the only thing that we care for its own sake is *our own* well-being or welfare, and that we can care about the well-being of any other being only instrumentally, as a means to

---

[15] Whereas our account implies that the spatial bias is irrational, like the bias towards the near future, Frances Kamm argues that there is justification for a spatial bias (2007: chs. 11 and 12).
[16] See Yudkowski, 2008: 105–7.

promoting our own well-being.[17] This view has been supported by a conceptual confusion, famously exposed by Joseph Butler (1726/1969), namely the confusion of thinking that the satisfaction that a person often feels when one of his or her desires is believed to be satisfied is *the object* of the desire. Whatever the object of a desire is—whether it be food and drink, exercise, knowledge, or company—there will be pleasure when the desire is believed to be satisfied. But this pleasure, which is *consequent* upon the (believed) satisfaction of a desire, must not be mistaken for an object of desire, i.e. what is desired. For instance, when you desire to eat, you are likely to feel satisfaction when you become aware of your eating, but this does not mean that the object of your desire is your eating as a means to your having this feeling of satisfaction. Similarly, when you desire that someone else gets something to eat and feel satisfied when you are made aware of this fact. Thus, the fact that this satisfaction contributes to your well-being does not show that the object of your desire concerns such a contribution to your well-being rather than simply that the other one gets something to eat.

When this confusion is out of the way, it can be seen that altruism—i.e. a sympathetic concern for the well-being of another for its own sake—is a *possible* element in our motivational repertoire, though it remains to be seen to what extent, if any, we are *in fact* altruists, and actually having this sympathetic concern. That is to say, we have seen that the fact that we feel satisfaction when things go well for individuals who are near and dear to us does not show that the object of our relevant desire is that things go well for these individuals in order that we ourselves will feel satisfied—in which case it would be an egoistic desire. But nothing so far said rules out that we are in fact egoists. That it is in fact the case that when we desire that things go well for someone else, we do not desire this for its own sake, but because it will in some way promote our own welfare. Thus, we might have a concern for its own sake only about the satisfaction of our own self-regarding desires—i.e. desires to the effect *we ourselves* obtain food, sex, recognition, etc.—and not at all about the satisfaction of the self-regarding

---

[17] This claim is too strong: someone who has some intrinsic concern for the well-being of somebody else would seem to qualify as an egoist if this concern is very small compared to the intrinsic concern for the well-being of the self. Note, however, that someone must have a conception of the well-being of other subjects in order to qualify as an egoist; an animal which is exclusively concerned about its own well-being because it lacks such a conception would not be an egoist.

desires of other beings, though we are aware that they do possess such desires.

However, such a picture of humans as pure egoists would sit ill with both everyday experience and evolutionary theory. From an evolutionary point of view, the most uncontroversial kind of altruism is *kin* altruism, i.e. altruism as regards our children, parents, siblings, and other relatives. Kin altruism is straightforwardly explicable in evolutionary terms, since each child has 50 per cent of each of its parents' genes, and siblings have on average the same percentage of genes in common. Consequently, caring about kin is caring about somebody who carries largely the same genes as we ourselves do. Again, although this is the evolutionary explanation or reason why we are altruistically disposed to our kin, it is not *our* reason or motive for being concerned about the weal or woe of kin—obviously, we do not possess any sensor which traces genetic relations. Instead, we seem to care about the welfare of our kin for its own sake chiefly because we have met them on a daily basis during longer periods and have grown accustomed to them. Such regular close encounters with individuals, especially in childhood, apparently tend to breed sympathy and liking for them, other things being equal, i.e. unless there are special reasons for averse feelings such as hostility, fear, disgust, etc.[18]

This mechanism of habituation could generate altruism also for non-kin whom we meet on a daily basis, since, as remarked, we do not register the presence or absence of closer genetic ties. For instance, children who grow up with some adopted children could become as attached to them as to their biological siblings. Thus, we have an explanation of how our altruism could spill over to individuals in our neighbourhood who are not our kin (cf. Joyce, 2006: 21–2).

It might seem, however, that such a wider range of altruism would be disadvantageous from an evolutionary point of view. This is because an altruistic disposition is likely to make altruists do favours to other

---

[18] Psychological egoists might insist that in these situations we do not exhibit concern about the well-being of another for its own sake; rather, we are concerned about relieving the distress *we ourselves feel* because we believe that another is distressed, and this is an egoistic concern. But why would we be distressed because we believe that another is distressed, unless we were concerned about the well-being of the other? Thus, we think that proposed egoistic motives often presuppose altruistic motivation. However, we agree with Stich et al., 2010, that neither evolutionary arguments nor social psychological experiments have *conclusively* established the presence of altruistic motivation. But we think that in conjunction with introspection and everyday observation they make up a very strong case in favour of it.

individuals, and this favouring tends to put these other individuals in better positions than the altruists themselves to survive and reproduce. Consequently, if altruism extends indiscriminately to individuals who ruthlessly exploit generosity shown to them, the altruists will be at a distinct evolutionary disadvantage.

But suppose instead that those who are benefited by altruists feel *gratitude*, which impels them to return the favours that the altruists have done to them. If not only altruism, but also this disposition to feel gratitude is widespread in a population, this population tends to do better than populations in which these motivational traits are rare or non-existent. For instance, if one animal that has been groomed gratefully returns the service, this mutually beneficial cooperation is likely to continue, with the result that the probability of the cooperators being infested by parasites decreases. Therefore, if we throw in something like a disposition to exhibit gratitude in the evolutionary mix, we have the beginnings of an explanation of why an altruism more wide-ranging than kin altruism would not be wiped out by evolutionary selection.

Still, those who receive favours, but do not return them, are likely to do better than grateful individuals who do return favours done to them, unless there is also a widespread disposition among benefactors, the grateful individuals, and third parties to react to ungrateful behaviour with *anger* or *aggression*, i.e. emotions that issue in tendencies to punish those who do not return favours. Consequently, it is reasonable to suppose that a disposition to feel proportionate anger on proper occasions is equally widely widespread. There are also other emotions that belong to this set of emotions which promote cooperation—a set which has been called *tit-for-tat*.[19] There is the *guilt* and *remorse* you feel when you yourself have acted wrongly, e.g. by not reciprocating when somebody has done you a favour; the *shame* you feel when you consider that you are—perhaps for this reason—inferior to others or fall short of an acceptable standard; the *forgiveness* you feel to other individuals who have acted wrongly, but have

---

[19] This term sometimes designates a simpler pattern of reactions, the pattern in which the response to a failure to return a favour does not include anger, but simply consists in the discontinuation of the doing of favours to the ungrateful individual. However, this simpler pattern seems of less evolutionary value, since it allows ungrateful individuals to get away too easily. That is why we focus upon the richer pattern.

shown guilt, remorse, and a desire to compensate for their wrongful behaviour.

Third-parties, who are disposed to react with anger or indignation towards individuals whom they observe failing to return favours done to them, would surely also be disposed to approve of those individuals who do return favours—as well as of those who performed the original altruistic act—and reward them in various ways. This is what is sometimes called *indirect reciprocity* (see e.g. Joyce, 2006: 31–3): the idea that the prospect of getting a 'good reputation' makes it more profitable for individuals to behave altruistically and to reciprocate.

It seems plausible to hypothesize that the emotions, which make up the tit-for-tat bundle, are bound up with our concept of *desert*. This is because when we feel gratitude towards somebody, we take it that this individual deserves a good return and praise; when we are angry at somebody, we see this individual as deserving to be punished and blamed; when we feel guilty, we feel that we deserve blame or punishment because we have acted wrongly in some way; when we are ashamed, we feel that we are more blameworthy than most; when we forgive someone, we withdraw our earlier view that they deserve blame and punishment for their wrongful behaviour, and so on. In other words, when we are in the grip of the tit-for-tat set of emotions, we regard individuals as deserving, or having deserved, the kind of treatment that we are, or were, inclined to deal them in virtue of having these emotions of gratitude, anger and so on.

Now desert is a consideration of *justice or fairness*: if you deserve some treatment then, other things being equal, it is just or fair that you receive it. It follows that individuals who are equipped with the tit-for-tat set of responses have some sense of justice or fairness. So, in contrast to David Hume, who famously taught that justice is an 'artifice', i.e. something which 'is not deriv'd from nature, but arises artificially, tho' necessarily from education, and human conventions' (1739–40/1978: 483), we believe that the concept of justice is a pre-cultural concept, of which traces can be found in some of the more social species of our mammalian ancestors. Likewise, possession of the concept of a right presupposes a sense of justice or fairness, since it implies that it is unjust or unfair to rob someone of something to which they have a right, and we have suggested that the concept of a right can also be traced to behavioural dispositions exhibited by our animal predecessors.

This connection to justice makes it still more evident that the tit-for-tat set is a set of *moral* responses. It lies close at hand to think that these justice-related responses, alongside altruism or sympathy (for others), qualify as moral responses because they are concerned with how others fare. It is plausible, though controversial, to claim that morality is a code that regulates one's relations to the well-being of *others*.[20] Since these responses survive only if they are widespread in a group, this feature of being widely distributed may also be part of what is meant by calling them moral responses.

The strength of the sense of justice or fairness can be tested in so-called *ultimatum games*. In these games there are two players, a proposer and a responder. The proposer proposes a certain division of some benefits, e.g. food or money. If the responder rejects the offer, neither the proposer nor the responder gets anything of the benefits. When the players are human, responders universally reject offers that would give them significantly less than an equal share. This is apparently because their feeling of being offended by an unfair division then becomes stronger than their desire for the benefit (remember, they will get nothing when they refuse the offer). Thus, we are willing to sacrifice benefits in order to protest against what we perceive to be unfair treatment. In the case of non-human animals, even animals closely related to humans, like chimpanzees, the evidence for their possession of a sense of justice is more ambiguous.[21]

When human beings acquired language, they could use their familiarity—with the phenomenon of feeling gratitude when somebody has rendered them a favour—as a model for a certain kind of promise, namely a promise or *offer* to benefit somebody in return if they have been benefited. Thereby, we have in our hands an instrument to strengthen a benefactor's trust that we shall return a favour, by promising to do so. Similarly, we could use our familiarity with the response of anger or vindictiveness as a model for a speech act of *threatening*: we could tell others that we shall hurt or harm them if they do not act in certain ways. Accordingly, speech acts such as these have the potential to augment the scope and frequency of our cooperative ventures. Also, by means of the

---

[20] This is not uncontroversial because some theorists claim that we have moral duties towards ourselves, and some believe egoism to be a possible theory of *morality* and not only of rationality.

[21] See Ch. 10 and Persson and Savulescu, 2008, for further discussion and references.

speech act of promising we can amplify the normative power of the reason to return a favour. If someone simply does you a favour, the benefactor may *deserve* a good turn. But if, before receiving this favour, you promised to pay the benefactor back in kind, then the benefactor has a *right* to this return, which provides you with a stronger reason to deliver it.

Tit-for-tat makes possible one form of cooperation which might be called *reciprocal*. It is a *consecutive* form of cooperation in which favours are first bestowed, and returned only later. This exchange of favours should be distinguished from another form of cooperation in which a number of agents more or less *simultaneously* contribute to a common goal. Hume gives a simple example of the latter: two oarsmen simultaneously rowing with one oar each (1777/1975: 306). Not only acquaintances, for whom we have developed trust and concern, but even strangers could be invited to this kind of *synchronic* cooperation since, as the case of the oarsmen clearly brings out, it does not pay for any party to try to cheat as this will be immediately detected, and all parties will lose out (the boat will go in circles and will never reach the destination). In such circumstances of observable or transparent participation, antecedent trust between the parties to a cooperative venture could be absent.

Things are different in so-called *prisoners' dilemma* in which the outcome depends upon somebody else's action, which could be simultaneous, but it is not transparent to you what the other party will do. In a standard illustration of prisoners' dilemma—which is admittedly artificial, but the cooperation problem it illustrates is nevertheless common in everyday situations—you and a comrade are separately questioned by the police. It is stipulated that it is best for you to confess if your comrade remains silent—you go free because you collaborated. Your comrade, however, gets twelve years of imprisonment. It is second best for you to be silent if he is also silent: say, you then get two years each, since the evidence against both of you will then be weak. But silence is the worst alternative if your comrade confesses, since you will then get twelve years, while he walks. Finally, if both of you talk, you will get ten years each. In this setup, rational self-interest tells each of you to confess, thereby avoiding what is worst for you (twelve years) and having a chance of getting what is best for you (zero years). But if both of you confess, you end up with the outcome which is third-best (ten years each), whereas if you had both been concerned about the welfare of the other and had trusted that he would have the same concern for you, both of you would have kept silent. Then you would have had what is second-best for both of you (two years each). Thus, your failure to collaborate, due to lack of concern for and trust in the other, will put both of you in a worse situation than you could have been in if you had collaborated.

An attempt at cooperation between two parties could instigate instances of synchronic cooperation from third parties: when loyal cooperators spot that somebody who has benefited from some cooperation defects, they could act together to punish him, for instance by excluding him from future cooperation. Obviously, awareness of the probability and possibility of such reactions from third parties discourages defection. Awareness that such reactions might be forthcoming will often be necessary to make the motivation to cooperate sufficiently strong, since, to repeat, human beings often are bent on getting the better of each other.

However, when synchronic cooperation involves innumerable agents, or is of long duration, it is usually harder to detect if someone defects or free-rides. Defection and free-riding are also more likely when the number of cooperators increase, for the reason that it is then less likely that they will personally know each other or have developed concern for and trust in each other. Furthermore, defection and free-riding are also facilitated in these cases by the fact that they harm others less by their non-cooperative behaviour, since the size of their contribution tends to decrease as the number of other contributors increases. This also makes it more probable that their contribution will not be necessary to achieve the goal; when their contribution to the goal becomes *negligible* or *imperceptible*, it could not be necessary for it. If their contribution would make no perceptible difference to the outcome, but involves a cost to them, it seems irrational for them to make it. For all these reasons, it is rational in these cases to have less trust or belief in the will of others to cooperate.

When the number of synchronic cooperators is smaller, altruism and trust are likely to be stronger. This could make cooperation possible, even when the behaviour of others is not open to inspection. The circumstances here are similar to those of consecutive, reciprocal cooperation where you first have to benefit another in order for a benefit to accrue to you later.

The range of our altruism is naturally limited to individuals who are close or similar to us in salient respects. Individuals who are close to us are often individuals in our neighbourhood whom we have grown to like and trust because we have encountered them on a daily basis for a long time. But our altruism also naturally extends to strangers who are similar to us in respects we consider important, e.g. individuals who share our dominant interests or ideals, or who have been afflicted by the same misfortunes as we have been.[22] On the other hand, there are factors that could block altruism towards people we regularly meet: for instance, the disgust we feel for homeless people whom we see everyday because they are dirty and unkempt could psychologically block our sympathetic concern for them. Obviously, conflicts of interests could do the same, by making us hostile or fearful.

There is an evolutionary reason why altruism does not extend indiscriminately to foreign and unfamiliar individuals: the risk that free-riders will exploit us would be too great. Suspicion against strangers is called for since, as we have repeatedly remarked, human beings often try to get the better of each other in the competition for resources. This is a plausible explanation of why *xenophobia* is a widespread characteristic of humanity. The spread of xenophobia indicates that, though humans throughout their history have lived out most of their lives in small, close-knit communities, these communities have frequently interacted with other small communities: if humans had rarely, or never, been in contact with strangers, a trait of suspiciousness towards strangers would be largely superfluous.

It should not be assumed, however, that the limits of our altruism are fixed once and for all, to exclude most strangers. We have already mentioned the mechanism of habituation, which makes it likely that we shall feel more sympathy for those who have in the past been strangers when we have more to do with them. So, globalization, including the fact that people nowadays travel and do business internationally, could weaken xenophobia.[23] We could also deliberately train ourselves in the art of empathizing and sympathizing with strangers by imagining what it would be like to be in their shoes,[24] and by repeatedly reminding ourselves of the superficiality and moral irrelevance of the conspicuous signs of someone's being alien, e.g. different skin colour, language, clothing,

---

[22] Cf. Frans de Waal: 'Empathy builds on proximity, similarity, and familiarity, which is entirely logical given that it evolved to promote in-group cooperation' (2010: 221).

[23] Of a piece with this is Steven Pinker's hypothesis that 'what inflated the empathy circle' in the late 18th century and brought about more humane societies, without slavery, duels, superstitious killings, savage punishments, etc., was 'the expansion of literacy', reading being 'a technology for perspective-taking' (2011: 175).

[24] This method plays a prominent part, e.g. in R. M. Hare's moral philosophy (1981).

and suchlike.[25] However, it would be unrealistic to expect quick and radical results by these means.

Both reciprocal and synchronic cooperation are beneficial to populations in which they are widely distributed. These populations tend to grow faster in number than populations in which they are more sparsely distributed. Even so, those who benefit most from these schemes of cooperation are inevitably the free-riders of these populations; therefore, the percentage of free-riders in cooperative populations will steadily increase. But, as Elliot Sober and David Sloan Wilson contend (1998: ch. 1), this need not be fatal to the total number of altruistic and cooperative individuals in different populations if we assume that the faster growing cooperative populations have opportunities of regrouping, with altruistic and cooperative individuals then tending to seek each other out. Although the percentage of altruists in their respective populations goes down, their total number in all populations may increase, since the populations of which they are members expand most. If altruists from different populations then have the opportunity to unite with others of their kind, their total number could continue to increase because the populations with a high rate of altruists are more successful. Thus, we would have an evolutionary explanation of how altruistic and cooperative dispositions, like tit-for-tat, will rise instead of diminish once they have acquired a foothold in a population, even though they are exploited by free-riders in that population.

All in all, we arrive at the following picture of our common morality and morally relevant psychology. We are primarily responsible for what we cause, in proportion to our causal contribution. What is morally most important is that we do not cause others rights-violating harms. Furthermore, we are psychologically myopic, disposed to care more about what happens to us and some individuals who are near and dear to us in the near future. We are capable of empathizing and sympathizing mainly with single individuals, and cannot empathize and sympathize with collectives in proportion to their number. Because we are equipped with the tit-for-tat set of responses, our parochial altruism enables us to engage in

---

[25] Of course, it is also possible to counteract the bad effects of limited altruism by introducing laws requiring us to help people in need, but this creates a self-interested reason to avoid discriminatory behaviour and is therefore not a way of extending our altruism, which is what we are now talking about.

consecutive, reciprocal cooperation, alongside synchronic cooperation, which itself does not presuppose altruism and trust as long as the participants are few enough to be able to keep an eye on each other constantly. But this check is not possible in modern societies with millions of citizens; here free-riding and antisocial individuals, who are bound to exist in larger societies on the basis of sheer probability, will find ample opportunity to escape notice and flourish.

It might be objected that this sketch of common-sense morality is at odds with some norms that have featured in the traditional morality of a majority of human societies around the world, e.g. norms prohibiting incest and cannibalism. These proscriptions do not seem to have to do with the well-being of other beings than oneself, which we have claimed to be a mark of moral norms. Our reply is that the reasons for upholding these proscriptions could concern the well-being of other beings than oneself, and that it is only if this is so that they could count as moral. One reason for holding that incest is wrong is that there is a high risk of it resulting in genetically defective offspring. Thus, it qualifies as a moral proscription if the causing of new beings to exist falls within the ambit of morality, as we have suggested. However, this does not apply to all cases of incest, such as those cases in which effective contraception is used. That the risk of inbreeding is not the customary reason for which incest has been regarded as wrong is shown by the fact that many people continue to think that incest is wrong even if they have been informed that effective contraception is used. It seems that these people think that incest is wrong because growing up with somebody in most people breeds feelings of a sort that make the thought of having sex with them repulsive. Presumably, the evolutionary reason why people have such feelings of revulsion is related to the risks of inbreeding, but *their* reason or motive for proscribing incest is nevertheless not such that it qualifies as a moral proscription in our vocabulary.

Our analysis of the proscription against cannibalism is similar. It is to be expected that human beings are naturally repelled by the idea of eating human corpses because it risks spreading diseases that might have been the cause of death. (This risk could be outweighed in societies that reside in environments in which there is a shortage of sources of protein.) In so far as this revulsion is what motivates the proscription, and it concerns only the eating of humans found dead, not the killing of humans to eat them, it is not a moral proscription, but rather a prudential proscription or recommendation. It is only if it is bound up with ideas, for example, about the well-being of the deceased, about harming or dishonouring their 'spirits', etc., that the proscription acquires a moral character.

According to our conception, then, morality is a set of rules for which these conditions hold: (1) they are about how other beings for whom something could be good or bad should be treated, and (2) they should be acceptable to the others as well as oneself in so far as they are capable of judging such rules. We think that something could be good or bad for a being only if it has consciousness at some point, but this idea is not part of the conception of morality. In metaethics, there are different views about the agreement of which (2) speaks: some are moral realists and think that this agreement is based on norms that are true independently of human attitudes, whereas others think that there is nothing beyond human attitudes that would ideally converge. Our conception leaves it open as to which of these views is true. It does suggest, however, that if moral relativism were to be true, because no agreement or convergence is forthcoming, this would constitute a revision of the commonsensical concept of morality.

3

Liberal Democracy

In the previous chapter, we described a set of psychological dispositions that we think are of particular importance for understanding our everyday moral actions and reactions. In the following chapters, we shall explore how fit or well equipped this psychological make-up makes us for life in modern societies with populations counting millions instead of hundreds, and with access to sophisticated science and technology of unprecedented power. Are we able to maintain the stability of our civilization with these kinds of behavioural dispositions coupled with such power, or shall we bring about its downfall? The type of modern society that we shall primarily consider is liberal democracy.

Liberal democracy is the type of society of which we and most of our readers are likely to be citizens. We propose to define liberal democracy ostensively or demonstratively as the form of government found in the nations of the European Union, the United States of America, Canada, Australia, New Zealand, Japan, and some other nations. We prefer a demonstrative definition because we want to present arguments which apply to these particular societies, not just to the societies, if any, which fit some abstract conception.[1] Many liberal democracies are affluent. These are the ones we shall focus on, since it is in them that scientific technology has its greatest impact and amplifies the problems that we shall discuss.

Still, we would like to give something of a general characterization of the ideal of liberal democracy which may only imperfectly fit the states mentioned. A fully liberal state is a state in which every citizen has equal rights and liberties which are as extensive as they could be, consistently

---

[1] Thus, it is irrelevant to object that these states are not real liberal democracies and, so, that a charge against them will not be a charge against *real* liberal democracy. For instance, it is irrelevant to the actual future of the Earth if real liberal democracies, which are never realized, would pay more heed to the environment and the interests of future generations.

with all others having the same rights and liberties. The requisite rights and liberties comprise equal rights before the law, equal rights to acquire property—thus, a liberal state has a market economy—and freedom of speech, press, assembly, and religion. A liberal state is ideally a state in which the citizens could freely determine the course of their own lives. The state interferes only when its citizens encroach upon the equal freedom of other citizens. It is natural to assume that the equal rights include an equal right to determine who will have the political power. Accordingly, a liberal state is typically a democracy in which every citizen by definition has a right to vote in general elections which settle who will govern.

The equal rights and liberties which constitute the political structure of a society are considered by liberal democratic thinkers, such as John Rawls, to be compatible with social and economic inequalities which are likely to result from a free market, so long as these inequalities can reasonably be expected to be to everyone's advantage, and are attached to positions open to all (1971: 60 ff.). Rawls does not think that social and economic inequalities which are beneficial to society—in particular, to its least advantaged members (1971: 83 and 302)—are *unjust* (1971: 62). But, according to an alternative form of egalitarianism, such socio-economic inequalities are unjust, though they could still be morally *justified*. When rights are exchanged for welfare as the cornerstone of morality, justice will be merely *one* moral consideration that should be balanced against other considerations, such as considerations of welfare or utility maximization. It might be that these other considerations outweigh considerations of justice, so that an outcome which is unjust is morally right or justified, all things considered. Such egalitarians obviously need a principle of welfare promotion alongside their principle of justice as equality, since otherwise they would have to say that equality at a low level of welfare is as good, morally speaking, as equality at a higher level. This is clearly counterintuitive.

It is important to emphasize the possibility of conflicts between justice and promotion of welfare for the reason that it brings out that, even if socio-economic inequality in a given society is morally justifiable because it is the outcome of a reasonable weighing of considerations of equality and welfare maximization against each other, there could nevertheless be *a* moral objection to it, namely to the effect that it is unjust. It is arguably unjust that, owing to shortcomings in respect of natural endowments, some will be worse off than others in a market economy. Even in a utopian society in which there is equality of opportunity in the sense that all have an equally good socio-economic background and education, and jobs and positions are open to all, those who by their genetic dispositions are less talented will be disadvantaged (as Rawls recognizes; 1971: e.g. 72–4). Because of their natural disadvantages, they will tend to end up in less well-paid jobs and will have lower social status. Some of them will even end up in institutions in which others take care of them. It is reasonable to think that this is as unfair as unequal social opportunities, since nobody is responsible for their genetically based deficiencies and, so, cannot deserve to be worse off because of them. Therefore, it might be concluded, justice requires that they be compensated for their genetic or natural deficiencies.[2]

Equality is of intrinsic value only to the extent that it is equality in respect of something that is of intrinsic value, like well-being. The relation of equality itself is not intrinsically valuable, so there is nothing intrinsically valuable about equality in respect of something which is not of intrinsic value; for example, there is nothing intrinsically valuable about our equal distance to some faraway planet.

Now, our well-being is dependent upon socio-economic factors as well as civil rights and liberties. Therefore, the most valuable equality—equality in respect of well-being in the widest sense of everything that makes our lives worthwhile or go well—will need to take into account economic factors as well as rights and liberties. There is no good reason to think that economic equality matters less to equality in respect of well-being than equality with respect to civil rights and liberties. But we could not achieve economic equality simply by removing all monetary rewards of the market economy, equalizing salaries, etc., since it is likely that such incentives promote prosperity and well-being overall—though we could probably do more to equalize the economic situation than we do at present without jeopardizing the promotion of well-being. In order to approach economic equality, we would rather have to equalize other factors that create economic differences, namely such factors as the varying intellectual and practical abilities of people.

---

[2] For an argument to this effect, see Persson, 2007b.

It follows that welfare egalitarians have moral reason to wish it were possible to enhance—e.g. by means of genetic engineering—the abilities of individuals who are disadvantaged by nature, just as they have moral reason to support equality of social opportunities. That is to say, they have reason to correct the effects of the natural lottery. For rough equality in both natural endowments and in terms of rights/liberties is necessary for rough equality of well-being—at least as long as human beings are not morally enhanced to become less selfish and more sensitive to egalitarian concerns.

We shall, however, zoom in on moral enhancement rather than on enhancement of other aspects of human nature. This is because our main target is the challenges that liberal democracies face because human nature is not designed to cope with a technological progress which has enormously increased the powers of action of humans, partly by boosting their number. Technological progress seems to have been instrumental in promoting the growth and spread of liberal democracy, by producing a profusion of wealth and welfare. Naturally, this profusion of wealth and welfare has accentuated problems of equality of distribution, but it is not clear that this is something that needs to threaten liberal democracy. As both ultimatum games and everyday experience show, people tolerate some amount of unfair inequality and, besides, some inequality may be seen as deserved and fair, as well as necessary to drive productivity.

We shall concentrate on what we think are the two greatest threats to liberal democracy: weapons of mass destruction and anthropogenic climate change and environmental degradation. As will emerge, both of these threats raise special difficulties for liberal democracies, and it is with them as problems internal to liberal democracy that we are particularly concerned. (Thus, we do not discuss weapons of mass destruction as an external threat to democracy from other states.) These problems may also interlock: diminishing natural resources resulting from detrimental climate change and environmental degradation could provoke wars with weapons of mass destruction over these resources. But global inequality also contributes to making climatic and environmental problems harder to solve for reasons that we shall outline in due course (see Chapter 7). Coping with these problems, we shall go on to argue in Chapter 10, requires a moral enhancement of humans.

4

Catastrophic Misuses
of Science

As explained in Chapter 2, it is generally much easier to harm than to benefit. It is quite easy for virtually anyone to do serious harm, say, to take a car and run down a number of people in a few seconds, but very few are ordinarily capable of saving as many lives in the same period of time. People can be killed at any point in their lives, but it is only in exceptional circumstances that we can save them from death and, as we have argued, even then we do not benefit them as much as we harm them were we to kill them. The comparative easiness of doing harm holds not only on the individual micro-level, but also on a macro-level. For instance, it is much more difficult to improve significantly upon comparatively well-ordered ecological systems on Earth than it is to damage them seriously. It may well be impossible for us ever to improve upon these ecosystems to the same degree as we are now damaging them. Hence, great caution is in place when we contemplate large-scale interventions with ecosystems, since unforeseen effects are likely, due to the enormous complexity of these systems. These unforeseen effects are likely to be mostly for the worse.

The fact that it is comparatively easier to harm than to benefit is a reason why misuses of scientific discoveries pose such an alarming threat. For the easiness to harm is magnified as our powers of action increase through technology, the power to harm always keeping its clear lead over an expanding power to benefit. During the last century our power to harm reached the point at which we can cause what might be called *Ultimate Harm*, which consists in making worthwhile life *forever* impossible on this planet. Since such a harm would prevent an indefinitely large number of worthwhile lives that would have been led in the future had it not occurred, its negative instrumental value is indefinitely high.

The expansion of scientific knowledge and technological prowess will put weapons of mass destruction in the hands of an increasing number of people. In so far as this is the case, this growth of knowledge will be instrumentally bad for us on the whole, by seriously augmenting the risk that we shall die, or be seriously harmed. For if an increasing percentage of us acquires the capacity to destroy an increasing number of us, it is enough if very few of us are malevolent or deranged enough to use this power for all of us to run a significantly greater risk of death and injury. It seems likely that within a decade or so the advance of scientific technology will make it possible for a single person with the relevant training to extinguish all higher life on Earth, and in a human population of more than seven billion it will not be long until there appears someone wicked enough to want to do so.

It should be noticed that, due to some of the moral shortcomings reviewed in Chapter 2, like our 'close range' altruism and numbness to greater numbers of sufferers, our inhibitions to use weapons of mass destruction are likely to be disproportionately weak in comparison to our inhibitions to kill single individuals with 'in-fight' weapons like machetes and axes, which cannot be used without close-up confrontations with blood and guts. It is psychologically harder and more revolting e.g. to slaughter ten people with a machete than to kill ten thousand or more people by dropping a bomb from an airplane.

The present technological know-how makes it possible for small groups, or even single individuals, to kill millions of us. Nuclear weapons are one well-known example, which have been feared since the 1950s. To make a nuclear bomb out of fissile material, such as highly enriched uranium or plutonium, seems not to be beyond the capacity of a well-organized terrorist group (cf. Ackerman and Potter, 2008: 412–14). If set off in a mega-city, such a bomb could kill millions of people and arouse panic among billions, causing medical disaster directly and social and economic catastrophe indirectly. Dozens of countries have poorly secured stockpiles of enriched uranium. Indeed, Richard Posner surmises that 'there may be enough plutonium outside secure military installations to furnish the raw material for 20,000 atomic bombs' (2004: 74). Some of this fissile material might fall into the lap of terrorist groups. A technological breakthrough might also enable non-state agents to enrich uranium. Another possibility is that terrorists will succeed in stealing nuclear weapons from a state. This could take place most easily in a period of political turmoil, such as during the coup against Soviet President Mikhail Gorbachev in 1991. Nor can one exclude the possibility of a nuclear state willingly supplying a terrorist group with nuclear weapons, e.g. Pakistan supplying al-Qaeda with such weapons. It is also conceivable that a terrorist group could trick one nuclear state into launching an attack upon another nuclear state, thereby provoking retaliation from the latter.

It may be asked whether any terrorist organization is prepared to use such devastating weapons. However, the former leader of al-Qaeda, Osama bin Laden, reputedly expressed interest in the acquisition of such weapons. There is evidence of attempts from this network to acquire them (see Ackerman and Potter, 2008: 420–2). It is also hard to see why a group like al-Qaeda, which was prepared to stage something on the scale of 9/11, would shrink back from the use of nuclear weapons against their enemies if they were in a position to use them effectively. On the contrary, they might be motivated to stage an act that would dwarf 9/11 to demonstrate their power (perhaps especially since Osama bin Laden has been killed, to avenge his death). Furthermore, such terrorist groups would hardly be deterred from doing so by the threat of nuclear retaliation, as states are prone to be, since they are evidently ready to die for their cause and become martyrs, and are at any rate difficult to hit because they are dispersed in small cells across the globe. It goes without saying that it is much more difficult to survey and control terrorist groups than much larger 'rogue' states. So, although the advance of scientific technology will predictably equip us with ever more effective methods of surveillance, this may not to be enough to keep up a reassuring level of security.

Another threat, which might be even scarier, is biological weapons. This threat is scarier for the reason that biological weapons are easier to fabricate than nuclear weapons—indeed, a single individual could do so. Chemical weapons, like the poisons ricin and sarin, are also easy to fabricate and, if distributed in a mega-city, they could kill tens of thousands.[1] But, while sharing the advantage of being relatively easy to produce with chemical weapons, biological weapons are more dangerous because they are contagious. Diseases could spread extensively before they are discovered, especially if their incubation time is relatively long, such as

---

[1] After having made several unsuccessful attempts to acquire nuclear weapons, the Japanese sect Aum Shinrikyo resorted to distributing sarin in Tokyo's underground, killing a dozen people.

a week or more. This is true of smallpox which kills one out of three infected. Biological weapons are also hard to control and outlaw because they are the downside of research which has the laudable aim of curing diseases; in other words, they involve products which have a dual use, both a beneficial and a harmful use.

For example, scientists in Australia were attempting to control a mouse plague by genetically engineering a virus, mousepox, which would leave mice sterile. However, they inadvertently produced a strain that was super-lethal, lethal in almost 100 per cent of mice.[2] Mousepox is similar to human smallpox, which in the 1970s was eradicated world-wide by a decades-long programme of vaccination. The study of the genetic modification of mousepox was published on the Internet, making it indiscriminately available. Genetic engineering of smallpox could create a new strain with a mortality of almost 100 per cent instead of 30 per cent, and with resistance against current vaccine. A small group of terrorists could fly around the world and deposit aerosolizers with fluids of this virus in airport terminals, underground stations, shopping malls, indoor stadiums, etc. Within a few minutes these aerosolizers could infect thousands of people at each location, most of whom would in their turn infect others, and so on. Since the incubation period of smallpox is one to two weeks, the disease would have spread extensively before it was even detected, and even after detection there would be no effective way of preventing further dissemination.

To provide a further illustration, a virologist has produced a genetically engineered Ebola virus that will enable researchers to mutate the virus to find out which of its genes and proteins cause its deadly effects. Such an invention could be a very valuable tool in the search for a cure and a vaccine, but it could also be put to the destructive use of increasing the infectiousness of the virus. Indeed, it has been reported that the Soviet Union biowarfare programme succeeded in doing something like this with a virus closely related to Ebola, Marburg Variant U (see Posner, 2004: 81).

Now, as we have suggested in Chapter 2, it appears rational to reject an intervention which is practically certain to produce some small improvement if there is also *some* risk, however small, of it bringing about a grave enough harm, even though the expected value of the intervention is

---

[2] Such a virus is unlikely to occur naturally, since it would be maladpative: it would wipe out itself by its high lethality.

mathematically greater than its expected disvalue. We gave a simple illustration of this phenomenon—big loss aversion—when we considered a choice of whether or not to participate in an activity in which the probability that you will gain two beneficial units is 99 per cent, but the risk that you will lose one hundred units is 1 per cent, e.g. an operation that will almost certainly correct a small defect of yours, but which could conceivably go seriously wrong, and damage you gravely, though this is very unlikely. Here the expected value of the possible improvement is nearly twice as big as the expected disvalue of the possible loss. Hence, according to standard expected utility theory it would be rational to undergo the operation, but to many of us this would seem far from rational. This has led to the proposal of alternatives to expected utility theory, like Kahneman and Tversky's 'prospect theory' (2000: pt. I), which aim to capture such reactions.

Granted, it is questionable to assign numerical values to benefits and harms, but our point does not turn upon such an assignment.[3] The point is that the difference in value between a small benefit and a big harm can be so great that no matter how high the probability of gaining the benefit, and no matter how small the risk of suffering the harm, as long as it is not perceived to be non-existent, most of us are not prepared to run the risk of suffering the harm in order to obtain the small benefit. If this is right, it is not a decisive objection that we are often incapable of estimating precisely the probability of a catastrophic harm; it is enough that we perceive it to be greater than zero in order reasonably to abstain from running the risk of it for the sake of gaining the small benefit.

A case in point might be CERN's Large Hadron Collider in Geneva. If people like the prominent British scientist Martin Rees (2003: 120–9) are right that operating it brings along a minimal risk of the formation of tiny black holes that could successively accrete surrounding matter until the entire planet is swallowed up, or of the formation of 'strangelets' that would

---

[3] It is questionable to assign numerical values to benefits and harms, since there would seem to be different *kinds* of benefits and harms in the sense that *no* greater (finite) amount of benefits (harms) of one kind can be as good (bad) as a smaller amount of some other kinds of benefit (harm). By different kinds of benefits and harms, we have in mind not only higher and lower pleasures of a traditional sort, such as the pleasures of poetry and fine arts versus gross sensual pleasures, but also cases in which there seems to be merely a great difference in intensity. Consider, for instance, a day of excruciating pain; it might seem worse to us than a lifelong very mild pain (see Temkin, 1996). If this is right, it is impossible to assign numerical values to these intensities of pain.

convert ordinary matter into strange matter, it would seem that we should do without its services, even if they certainly bring along some benefits.

Our situation with respect to further technological advances might be analogous to such situations in which a small gain that is virtually certain goes with a minimal risk of a catastrophic loss. That is to say, these advances will almost certainly lead to small increases of our already high quality of life—more or better food, better medicines and health care, better means of transport and communication, etc.—but at the cost of marginally increasing the risk of a large number of deaths in the near future. Such a destructive outcome might occur either through someone's deliberate misuse of these advances, or through ignorance or negligence of some possible outcomes. To exemplify the latter risk, think of synthetically created organisms escaping into the wild and outcompeting naturally occurring organisms (see Douglas and Savulescu 2010).

The thought that the risk of grave harms matters more than they come out as doing according to standard expected utility theory may be one thing that people have in mind when they appeal to the so-called *precautionary principle*. When generally stated, this principle requires that we should adopt extra precautions, or a margin of safety, in dealing with the risks of grave harms. The precautionary principle is however frequently invoked—indeed, too frequently in our opinion—so, it would be unwise of us to claim to be explicating the one and only principle with this name.

There is another possible aspect of the precautionary principle to which we have also alluded in Chapter 2. This is the aspect that has to do with the fact an arbitrary interference in a functioning system, like an organism or ecosystem, is much more likely to damage it than to improve it, because the ways in which such a system could be damaged are indefinitely more numerous than the ways in which it could be improved. Consequently, when we interfere with well-adapted organisms and ecosystems, we need very extensive knowledge to be able to make, with reasonable certainty, interferences that enhance their functioning rather than occasion them to malfunction.[4]

---

[4] So, we believe that it is rational to keep our spontaneous big loss aversion. In contrast, we think that we should probably try to get rid of our big gain attraction. It might not cause us much harm in a natural environment, but it could easily ruin us when we are surrounded by casinos and betting companies.

Many human interferences with the environment have undoubtedly been ill-considered and harmful. For example, Jared Diamond supplies plenty of instances in his review (2005) of civilizations that have collapsed. The precautionary principle might reasonably be taken to imply that we highlight the fact that it is far easier to damage than to enhance, and therefore we should not interfere radically with a stable system, unless we have taken great pains to exclude unforeseen effects and to ensure that the effects that we have foreseen are decisively good. But it is the first aspect—the disproportionate weight of great harms—rather than this second aspect of our understanding of the precautionary principle that is of most relevance at the moment.

The enormous size of the populations of modern liberal democracies by itself makes it likely that they will contain minority groups or single individuals bent on intentionally misusing the formidable powers afforded by advanced scientific technology. But this problem is compounded by one of the hallmarks of liberal democracies: tolerance towards people of different ethnicity and culture, together with the migration of people that modern means of transportation have made possible.

This is a new phenomenon. Historically, human societies have tended to be more culturally homogeneous than contemporary liberal democracies. This appears to be so chiefly for two reasons. First, human beings are strongly disposed to conform to the standards of their society. When they grow up, children do not merely acquire knowledge of the cultural traditions of their society, its language, religion, etc.—most of them readily adopt these traditions and regard them as superior to alternative customs (if they were ever to come across any). Secondly, in the past there was comparatively little mobility between one society and another: as a rule, people stayed put in the society into which they were born. To be sure, it has frequently happened in the course of history that one society has conquered another, and the population of the latter has been incorporated into the former (in so far as it was not exterminated), but then the culture of the conquered people tended to be suppressed or subordinated, so that the conquering society would remain relatively culturally homogeneous. In contrast, modern liberal democracies are avowedly *multicultural*; they are as a point of ideology tolerant of cultural diversity. They allow minorities to cultivate different political and religious ideals in their midst. This brings along an inescapable risk that some of these minorities will contain subgroups that are prepared to resort to violence to promote ideologies that oppose democracy and liberalism. Modern scientific technology is liable to provide them with ever more powerful weapons to further their causes.

To be sure, the progress of science also equips liberal democracies with more effective means of surveillance. Their intelligence agencies may be able monitor all electromagnetic transmissions—phone calls, email communication, etc.—which involve their societies, unless they are unbreakably encrypted. They could survey public places by CCTV and record face-to-face conversations. Digitization and computerized data processing make possible the storage of an overwhelming mass of such information about individual citizens. When the aim is to protect national security, The Foreign Intelligence Surveillance Act of the United States authorizes such surveillance on the basis of a suspicion which is weaker than is requisite in normal criminal investigations (see Posner, 2004: 232). But if authorities employ these wide-ranging means of intelligence, they seem to set aside a right to privacy, which is one of the characteristics of a liberal state, and turn it into something uncomfortably like the totalitarian state depicted in George Orwell's novel *Nineteen Eighty-Four*. It might be feared that, if citizens are constantly under surveillance, there is a risk is that they will become anxious conformists rather than the self-reliant and independent individualists of whom J. S. Mill speaks so eloquently in his liberal classic *On Liberty* (1859/1978).

Whether or not this surveillance of citizens can be morally justified largely depends upon whether they should be accorded a moral right to privacy, i.e. a moral right that outsiders do not gain information about the right-holding citizens that they do not want anyone but themselves and a select few to possess. But the existence of such a moral right is doubtful. Even such a staunch defender of moral rights as Judith Thomson denies its existence (1990: 280).

Indeed, it is hard to see how you could have a moral right against others that they do not acquire or sustain beliefs about you, whatever their content. The reason is that in itself their acquisition of beliefs about you need not involve any change of your state, but only in their state. In contrast, the *means* they use to acquire beliefs about you, or the *use* to which they put these beliefs could affect you and, so, could violate your moral rights. This is why other moral rights, like property rights, could provide some of the protection that a right to privacy would provide. For instance, if you own a house and, thereby, have a right that others do not enter it without your permission, you could normally ensure the privacy of some of your activities by performing them inside your house. Given the actual conditions of the world, the property that you have will place restrictions upon the amount of information that others could legitimately acquire about you.

Consequently, as people have acquired more property in the course of history, their possibilities of enjoying privacy have expanded. The amount of privacy that average people in contemporary Western societies enjoy is probably unique in the history of humankind. Throughout most of their history, people in general have lived in conditions in which there was little space or need for privacy. For instance, in hunter-gatherer societies a search for privacy was regarded as a sign that you had devious designs, and in medieval Europe people, without embarrassment, defecated and had sex in front of others. This might lead one to think that the moral right to privacy that affluent people today feel that they have is a reflection of the circumstances in which they are accustomed to live, the protection of property that they own, customs that have happened to arise, and so on.

To bring home the point that the permissibility of acquiring some piece of information depends upon the means used to acquire it, imagine that some of your fellow-citizens developed means of acquiring extensive information about you without violating any of your moral rights (other than an alleged right to privacy), without affecting you or your property in any noticeable way. For instance, imagine that they developed an X-ray eyesight so that they could see you naked without removing your clothes, a hearing so sharp that they could eavesdrop on you by merely walking past your house, or a power of telepathy that enabled them to read your mind merely by looking you in the eye. It would then be unreasonable of you to claim that you have a right against these people to ensure that they do not perform such everyday acts as looking at you, walking past your lodgings, or looking you in the eye. It might be nice of them if they did not do so, but it cannot be required of them as a matter of right. The actions mentioned are ones that they would have every right to perform if they were not endowed with any 'super-sense', but their super-senses merely allows them to gain more information about you, and this is a change only in them, not in you. However, in actual circumstances such information cannot be acquired without the use of means that would violate some of your rights, by removing your clothes, breaking into your house, etc. Since we have rights that those acts, which are normally necessary means to acquire certain types of information about us, should not be performed, it might wrongly be inferred that we have a right against the information acquisition in itself, which would protect us *whatever* the means of acquisition employed.

It might be objected that, by gaining or possessing certain types information about you, strangers could cause you distress, embarrassment, fear, etc.—if you become aware that they were gaining or possessing this information—and that this is an (unpleasant) change in your state. But inducing such 'belief-mediated' distress does not violate any moral right of yours, as Thomson argues (1990: 253–7). If it did, you could acquire very extensive rights against others just by being extremely sensitive about what others think about you. All the same, people with super-senses could be kind enough not to put to use their super-senses to acquire information about you that would distress or embarrass you. Likewise, a state could be generous enough to grant its citizens a *legal* right not to be subject to means which, though not morally right-infringing in themselves, are used for the purpose of acquiring information about these citizens that would distress or embarrass them—albeit the citizens could not demand this as a matter of moral right. That is, there could be legal rights that do not correspond to any moral rights, but which merely protect the common interests of people.

Returning to the example of people with super-senses, there could be circumstances in which they would be perfectly justified in putting their senses to use. Imagine that they have some reason to believe that their neighbours are conspiring against them. Then they could walk past their neighbours' lodgings justifiably to eavesdrop on them, or look them in the eye to mind-read them. This could be justifiable, even if the suspicion is rather weak, and only provides a weaker reason than that usually required to put aside a moral right, e.g. the right to property by breaking into their neighbours' houses. Similarly, even a rather remote probability of a grave threat to a society could justify surveillance of its citizens by the authorities if this could be done without infringing their (other) moral rights. It takes a stronger reason to justify intelligence which involves infringements of such rights, say, by breaking into people's houses. But the threat to the safety of a society could be large enough to justify even this because security of life and limb is a matter of preventing infringements of other, more stringent moral rights. If it is necessary that other moral rights be infringed to obtain information, which is indispensable to safeguard to a requisite degree a more stringent moral right, then this infringement is justifiable.

To put the argument in our favoured terminology of benefits and harms, it is necessary to keep in mind the disproportionate importance of great harm noted in Chapter 2. If there is an epistemic probability larger than zero that such greater harm could occur, then it could be morally justifiable to reduce this probability by means that certainly impose minor inconveniences upon an indefinite number of people, although the sum of the expected minor harms of applying these means is greater than the expected benefit of reducing the probability of the great harm. It seems reasonable to hold that a general restriction of a legal right to privacy to which we have grown accustomed is such a small sacrifice that we could learn to live with it if this is necessary for safety of life and limb. The same goes for a more extensive surveillance of people who voluntarily take on certain roles such as to work with dangerous substances, if general surveillance of them is not enough to attain an acceptable level of public security. But this is a matter of balancing different interests that cannot be done objectively, so there is no way of showing what amount of surveillance is morally acceptable.

Although liberal democracies could be justified in curtailing an existing legal right to privacy in response threats to the safety of their citizens, there is, however, a risk that this curtailment could become too drastic, or unfairly discriminatory. Suppose that there is a major terrorist attack, say, something like the one that occurred in New York City on September 11, 2001, in which almost 3,000 people died. The horror of such an attack could make the public grossly exaggerate the risks of future attacks of a similar kind, especially if this reaction is fuelled by politicians and media. In a cross-national study made in the United States a couple of years after 9/11, US citizens on average estimated that the risk of their being seriously harmed by a terrorist attack in the next year was 8.27 per cent. Even though there is no way of accurately determining what the actual risk of this was, this figure is surely an absurd exaggeration. It would mean that in the next year there would occur terrorist attacks that would harvest some 25 million US lives. The occurrence of a terrorist attack which claimed 3,000 lives cannot make it reasonable to expect such a calamitous outcome. The risk of a US citizen dying in a motor vehicle accident in 2001 was only 0.015 per cent, and that year a US citizen was statistically fifteen times as likely to die in such an accident as in a terrorist attack (see Sunstein,

2007: 40, 43).[5] Terrorists could not kill millions of US citizens in a year, unless they were in possession of powerful weapons of mass destruction, and then one would wonder why they did not use them instead of enacting the far less lethal 9/11 attack.

The explanation of this exaggeration of the risk of dying in a terrorist attack after September 11 is presumably that human beings are subject to the availability bias. For a considerable period of time after 9/11, images of the two airplanes flying into the two towers of the World Trade Center and their consequent collapse were readily available to the imagination of US citizens to inflate their fear of similar terrorist attacks in the future. But there is a further mechanism which probably helped to cause this emotional upsurge. When identifiable human agents rather than natural causes, like earthquakes and floods, are responsible for harm, emotions like anger, indignation, and vindictiveness are prone to be directed against the agents who are responsible.[6] They would not have been directed at a natural phenomenon such as an earthquake or meteorite had it caused the collapse of the two towers. These emotions readily spread to the ethnic groups of which the perpetrators are members. We noted in Chapter 2 a latent xenophobia in human nature, and it does not take much for it to flare up. It is clear that, if the public's feelings of fear and anger at some ethnic group are inflated, this might pave the way for the introduction of measures that discriminate against citizens of this group.

Consequently, the tendency of liberal democracy to turn less liberal under terrorist threats might escalate far beyond justification. The US presidential authority to detain suspected terrorists for years without trial in camps outside US territory, like Guantánamo, and the use of 'extended interrogation', with brutal elements such as waterboarding, are plausibly

---

[5] Ironically, the exaggerated fear of dying in a terrorist attack like the one on 9/11 led to more US citizens dying in car accidents because they chose to drive instead of flying. Gerd Gigerenzer estimates that in the year following 9/11 'fifteen hundred Americans died on the road in the attempt to avoid the fate of the passengers who were killed in the four fatal flights' (2008: 98).

[6] Because of the so-called hindsight bias, they might also be unfairly directed at security personnel who failed to prevent the agents of harm. This bias is the phenomenon that if an improbable event happens, it afterwards seems more probable. After an event has happened, we might say 'I knew it would happen', though we would certainly not claim knowledge in advance. Likewise, after September 11 the terrorist attack might seem more probable and, thus, security personnel might seem more responsible for not having foreseen and prevented it.

cases in point.[7] Liberal democracies might also introduce far-reaching travel restrictions which would effectively lock out foreigners belonging to certain ethnic groups. For instance, in 2006 the United States accepted only 202 refugees from Iraq, while Sweden, which took no part in the invasion of Iraq, and whose population is more than thirty times smaller (9 million compared to over 300 million), accepted more than 8,000. The least dishonourable reason for this US low acceptance would seem to be self-protection, the US authorities' fear of admitting potential terrorists, but this reason must be balanced against a moral obligation to alleviate suffering that follows in the wake of a war you initiate for no compelling reason.

On the other hand, some anti-terrorist measures are clearly justifiable, for instance regulations that concern people whose work or study has to do with lethal pathogens. Examples might be *The Public Health Security and Bioterrorism Preparedness and Response Act*, which directs the FBI to conduct background investigations of scientists who have access to certain pathogens and toxins, and the part of *The USA Patriot Act* which forbids, for instance, aliens, who are nationals of countries considered to be supporters of terrorism, to have access to such substances (see Posner, 2004: 226). It also seems justifiable to suppress the (legal) right of free speech as regards the publication of information concerning the manufacture of lethal pathogens and toxins—the mousepox study we cited above is a case in point. Such information should be classified, like military information. The right of free speech is a right to which there are many other exceptions: defamation, child pornography, unauthorized publication of copyrighted material, hate speech, and indecent speech on radio and television (see Posner, 2004: 230). A further exception could well be to prevent future terrorist attacks and, thereby, a public overreaction to such attacks that would lead to even more Draconian measures. Closer surveillance of citizens, who have visited countries in which there are known to be terrorist training camps and restrictions on immigration from them, might also be justified.

To sum up, in our globalized and culturally mixed world there is not just an actual threat of increasingly devastating acts of terrorism to which liberal democracies must protect themselves; there is also a risk of an

---

[7] We believe that torture and torture-like methods are justifiable only in the most extreme cases, when they are clearly indispensable to stave off impending threats to lives.

irrationally overblown fear and vindictiveness called forth by such attacks, as a result of factors like the availability bias and ingrained xenophobia. We have suggested that the actual threat of acts of terrorism, with potential access to weapons of mass destruction, could justify a liberal democracy's becoming less liberal, by curtailing the citizens' legal right to privacy and to freedom of speech even if the risk of such acts is quite small because the harm that they could cause could be catastrophic. Even people who believe in moral rights should be able to see the force of this case because there is no moral right to privacy. It should be clear, however, there is no objectively right way of making such weighings between different rights or interests. But liberal democracies must be on their guard to ensure that factors like the availability bias and latent xenophobia do not make them overreact and constrain the freedom of certain groups of its citizens more than is warranted. Such overreaction seems especially likely when acts of terrorism occur against a background of possible future acts of terrorism on an even larger scale.

Another consequence of the fact that we labour under the availability bias is that we are likely to overestimate the probability of specific threats, which are similar to those we have already experienced, e.g. the probability that future terrorist attacks will take a shape that has to do with aviation rather than, say, with nuclear or biological weapons. Consequently, precautions undertaken may be unjustifiably selective (for instance, there are ever more rigorous security checks at airports, but very few of them at railway stations). As even our brief review indicates, the threats are more multifarious than we might initially be inclined to imagine. Finally, it should be emphasized that the threat of terrorists, or other warped individuals, with access to weapons of mass destruction is in all probability not a passing threat, but one that that will persist, or grow, as long as scientific technology is at least as sophisticated as it is today.

5

Responsibility for Omissions

The growth of our powers of action due to the inventions of scientific technology makes it more important to realize the untenability of the act-omission doctrine of common-sense morality, described in Chapter 2. The reason is that, as our powers of action increase, so does the range of what we let happen through failures to use these powers. It is a conceptual truth that we can *let* something happen, or *allow* it to happen, by omitting to prevent it, only if it is in our power to prevent it, and we are aware that it is in our power. We currently have a power to affect states of affairs globally and far into the future to an extent that we have never had before. Consequently, it is now more important than ever for us to realize that the act-omission doctrine is erroneous. For we would then realize that much of what we have let happen because we have tacitly assumed the truth of this doctrine, and because of our limited altruistic motivation, is morally unjustifiable.

Many people have argued in various ways that the act-omission doctrine is unjustifiable. One way of doing so takes as its point of departure the fact that something could at the same time be both an action of ours and something that we let happen by omitting to act.[1] Suppose that you are feeling a spasm coming on in your arm. Suppose also that you know that if you do not quell the spasm, which you know that you could do, say, by flexing some muscles in your arm, it will cause you to pull the trigger of a loaded gun in your hand and shoot a victim, Vic, dead. If you let the spasm run its course, by omitting to flex those muscles, you let yourself kill this person. You will then simultaneously act (fire the gun and shoot Vic) and let something happen, namely, that

---

[1] For a fuller exploration of this argumentative strategy, see Persson, 2004. Kamm provides an elaborate defence against some earlier attempts—e.g. by Rachels, 1975—to undermine the act-omission doctrine (1996: pt. I). That is why we do not make use of these attempts.

you perform this act of shooting Vic, by omitting to flex your muscles. Are you then, according to the act-omission doctrine, acting as wrongly as you would be were you intentionally or consciously to shoot Vic dead, or permissibly as you might be were you to let Vic die from a cause external to you?

On the one hand, when you let yourself shoot Vic, you seem to be acting as wrongly as when you intentionally or consciously shoot him, for in both cases you do shoot him. Furthermore, this would not have occurred if you had not had a certain attitude to it: you would not have done so, unless you had intended, or accepted, the outcome that Vic be shot by you. On the other hand, when you let yourself shoot and kill him, by letting the spasm run its course, you seem to be acting in way that could not be more wrong than when you let an external natural force, say, a branch stirred by the wind, pull the trigger, with the result that Vic is shot dead. For a spasm is also a natural force, and how could it make any moral difference whether a natural force, which you allow running its course, is internal or external to your body? But if letting yourself kill Vic would come out both as wrong as your intentionally or consciously killing Vic, and not more wrong than your letting something external to your body kill Vic, it follows that intentionally or consciously killing cannot be more wrong, or harder to justify morally, than letting something external to you kill him. However, that contradicts the act-omission doctrine.

If this doctrine is false, it would be as wrong of us, say, to let misery go on in the developing world, by failing to aid, as to cause the same amount of misery there, other things being equal, i.e. the cost to us being the same in both cases. However, we shall not press this point, since it has been forcefully argued by others,[2] and it is not at the centre of the issue that concerns us, namely the ability of liberal democracy to cope with threats created by scientific technology. But it is linked to the problem of climate change and environmental destruction. Obviously, an important key to this problem is to control population growth, which mostly occur in developing countries. Thus, support of family planning in these countries is essential. Moreover, help to developing countries should also include helping them to develop in sustainable ways. If the global emission of carbon dioxide is to be radically reduced, future economic development in

---

[2] See e.g. Singer, 1993: ch. 8; and Unger, 1996.

these countries cannot be driven by fossil fuels as it has been in the affluent countries. But developing countries cannot afford to put in use alternative energy resources without aid from affluent countries.

However, it is a general point that we particularly wish to underline: the more extensive the powers of action that we possess thanks to scientific technology, the greater our moral responsibility. More precisely, if we are aware that it is in our power to prevent some harm, and we refrain from so doing, we could be as responsible for its occurrence as we would be had we knowingly caused it. We would be as responsible for the harm if the circumstances are such that it would be as little costly to us (and others) to prevent it as to avoid causing it. If this is right, people in affluent liberal democracies are more responsible and blameworthy for the misery in developing countries than they commonly think they are because it seems undeniable that they could prevent a lot of it at very little cost to themselves.

This reasoning does not take into consideration whether people in affluent countries have actively made any causal contribution to the misery in developing countries. It may be argued that, to a degree which is admittedly hard to estimate, people in developed countries *have* in fact actively contributed to the plight of people in the developing world, by having exploited their natural resources, not only in the colonial era, but even in our day, by imposing unfair trading conditions and by supporting incompetent or corrupt political regimes. Such considerations would supply these affluent countries with a further reason, consisting in a special obligation, to give aid to the developing world. The size of this aid should then be proportionate not only to the misery that they have caused, but also to the profit they have earned. Although we cannot elaborate these facts about global inequality, we want to note them in passing, since they are pertinent to the environmental and climatic problems that we shall soon discuss.

Let us also note that the developed nations have to a large extent shirked their responsibilities with respect to the developing world. For instance, in 2008 only five countries (Sweden, Luxembourg, Norway, Denmark, and the Netherlands) had reached the modest goal that the United Nations set decades ago of aid amounting to 0.7 per cent of a country's GDP. The average for OECD-nations was 0.47 per cent; the two biggest world economies at the time, the United States and Japan, were located at the bottom, at around 0.2 per cent. One factor behind the reluctance to aid is presumably the hold that the act-omission doctrine has on our minds. Another factor is probably our parochial altruism and emotional numbness to numbers of victims that we noted in Chapter 2. To repeat, with the expansion of our powers of action, these propensities of ours become an increasingly serious moral shortcoming, since this expansion means that the scope of the harm that we could prevent grows. The same goes for our built-in bias towards the near future because, as our capabilities of action increase, the effects of our actions will extend further into the future, stretching across periods of time that this bias inclines us to downplay. This fact will be of great importance when we move on to discuss the impact that our consumerist lifestyle has on the global environment and climate, since this is an impact which is likely to extend over centuries.

There is another aspect of the conception of causally-based responsibility, encapsulated in the act-omission doctrine that should be mentioned. Our consumerist lifestyle has grave climatic and environmental consequences because it takes place in immensely populous societies in which innumerable individual agents together cause these consequences. The causal impact of each agent upon the climate and environment thereby becomes unnoticeable or imperceptible. Consequently, the causally-based responsibility of each agent is diluted to the point of becoming negligible. It follows that the causally-based conception of responsibility carries the peculiar implication that individuals could eschew responsibility for the production of some harmful effect by joining up with a sufficient number of other agents to produce it. This is surely objectionable. Imagine that several agents join forces and cause Vic's death by each giving him such a small dose of a drug that by itself is not harmful. Then, if each of them is aware of what the others are doing, it is arguable that each of them is as responsible for Vic's death as they would have been had they caused it single-handedly. They are as responsible in the former case because they have intentionally caused Vic's death by joining up with similarly motivated agents instead of by single-handedly applying some other means, such as a large dose of the drug. It would be absurd to claim, as the notion of causally-based responsibility allows us to do, that each of them is only responsible for giving Vic a harmless dose of the drug, which might not be wrong at all.

Compare two different situations comprising, say, 1,000 agents and 1,000 victims (cf. Parfit, 1984: sect. 29). In the first situation each agent gives one victim a lethal dose. In the second situation, having agreed with the other 999 agents about how to act, each agent gives each of the 1,000 victims 1/1,000 of this dose, an amount that is perfectly harmless. In both situations the outcome is the same: 1,000 victims die of poisoning. Surely, each agent is morally responsible for as much harm in the second situation as in the first. The dwindling causal contribution of each member of a collective is a feature that should be kept in mind because it aggravates the cooperation problems that will be considered in the next chapter.

There is an analogous dilution of the responsibility for omissions which, according to the conception of causally-based responsibility, is considerably weaker to begin with. This dilution kicks in when we could collectively, but not individually, help some victims, but so many of us omit doing our bit that the individuals in need are not helped. The situation of affluent people as regards aid to the developing world might be of this kind. But here the number of agents involved is so large that the contribution of each is likely to be negligible, and along with it the causal responsibility for each failure to provide aid. This could be a significant part of the explanation of why the affluent have dragged their heels in providing aid to the developing world.

The situation just sketched should be distinguished from a similar, but relevantly different situation. It has been observed that individuals are less inclined to help someone in need when they are one of several bystanders, each of whom could *single-handedly* help the victim, than if each individual were the only bystander around. This situation is sometimes lumped together with the one described in the preceding paragraph under the label 'bystander apathy'. But they are relevantly different. In the situation in which each bystander is capable of helping single-handedly, there is no dilution of individual causal responsibility: each is responsible for a failure to help, as long as there is no justification for thinking that anyone else is better placed to help. If there are other, equally capable bystanders around, we often hope or wish that they will incur the cost of helping. If they fail to do so as well, we could find comfort in the thought that we are not morally worse than they are. But here we are all equally, and *fully*, responsible for a failure to help, not just responsible for contributing a 'bit' to such a failure as in the case earlier considered.

In this chapter, we have pointed to the great harmfulness of the conception of causally-based responsibility underlying the acts-omission doctrine in today's world of increasing powers of action. As our powers have grown through the advance of technology, we become responsible for the many millions we could help, both now and in the future, through the better deployment of that technology. It is to future generations, and their fate at the hands of climate change, that we now turn.

6

The Tragedy of the Commons

The fact that contemporary societies consist of millions of citizens makes it harder to solve the problem of cooperation known as *the tragedy of the commons* (see Hardin, 1968). This problem is similar to the prisoners' dilemma considered in Chapter 2, but it gets its name from another kind of example which is akin to the ones we shall henceforth concentrate upon, namely anthropogenic climatic and environmental changes, primarily caused by the overconsumption of resources and wasteful lifestyle of modern affluent societies.

These climatic and environmental problems include a global warming which, according to most experts, is to a considerable extent a result of the human emission of greenhouse gases like carbon dioxide, methane, and nitrous oxide. Carbon dioxide is released by the burning of fossil fuels, that is, oil, coal, and natural gas. The burning of tropical forests also releases carbon dioxide. As forests absorb more carbon dioxide than they emit, deforestation reduces this absorption, which further exacerbates the greenhouse effect. Since greenhouse gases do not block sunlight, but do reflect heat that is radiated skywards from the Earth's surface, an increase of these gases in the atmosphere will cause a rise of global temperature. In turn, this will lead to a progressive melting of the huge ice sheets on Greenland and Antarctica that will make the sea level rise, so that coastal lowland, some of which is densely populated, e.g. Bangladesh and the Netherlands, threatens to be inundated. The melting of these ice sheets will reduce the albedo effect, i.e. the reflection of sunlight from these areas, and this will stoke up the temperature boost. Another effect of the temperature boost is that methane could be released from permafrost regions and from ocean bottoms. This would further spur the greenhouse effect, since methane traps heat twenty times as effectively as carbon dioxide. Also, if the global temperature rises by 4°C, around 80 per cent of the trees in tropical forests will die and release carbon dioxide, which is likely to raise the temperature even further.

The warmer the atmosphere, the greater its water-retention capacity and water vapour in the atmosphere adds to the greenhouse effect. Because there will be less precipitation, there will be more droughts and desertification in some places, e.g. in Africa and South-east Asia, rendering agriculture more difficult for people who are already poverty-stricken. It is true that a temperature rise is also likely to open new land for agriculture, for instance on Greenland, but having people migrate from Africa and Asia to Greenland would create enormous logistic and other problems. Tropical diseases like malaria will also spread and afflict more people. However, in some parts of the world there might also be a troublesome opposite effect on temperature. The melting of the ice cover of Greenland might dilute the salty water of the North Atlantic to the extent that the Gulf Stream will flow more directly north along the North American coast, with the result that it no longer heats the Scandinavian peninsula. The temperature in these areas could drop by 5°C or more, making agriculture more difficult.

It would be bad enough if significant increases in temperatures occurred gradually, but it cannot be excluded that there is a tipping point at which the temperature will jump abruptly. The global temperature has been known to increase by as much as 8°C in a decade; to put this in perspective, it should be mentioned that the temperature difference between the present time and the last ice age is at most 5°C (and it occurred slowly, over several thousand years). The causes behind climatic changes are not sufficiently well known to rule out that such dramatic temperature jumps will occur again if greenhouse gases continue to be emitted at their current rate. Abrupt climate changes are worse than gradual ones, since there is less time to adjust agriculture to them.

Apart from its impact upon humankind, global warming will also have drastic effects upon the habitats of a lot of the flora and fauna of the world. This is especially true of the flora and fauna that are adapted to the cold climate close to the polar caps. Flora and fauna are also put under pressure by the loss of natural habitats, which is caused by a more direct human influence on them: more than half of the original boreal and tropical forests and wetlands of this planet has been lost to cities, roads, farmlands, golf courses, and so on. Thirty per cent of the coral reefs have been severely damaged by overfishing, higher temperatures, and pollution. In the wake of this destruction of habitats, there is an accelerated extinction of species of animals and plants. It is not possible to specify precisely the rate of this drainage of biodiversity—even the number of species existing on Earth is a matter of controversy (as is indeed the concept of a biological species itself). But some reputable biologists, like E. O. Wilson (2002: 98–100), take the current extinction rate to be between 10,000 to 1,000 times as fast as the natural one, which would occur if there were no human interference. It is not known what effect this loss of biodiversity will have on human welfare, aside from the frustration of those who take an interest in this biodiversity for its own sake. But to people, like the present authors, who believe that all sentient organisms have moral status, the extinction of such organisms is in itself morally bad, apart from any consequences on humankind.

A further environmental problem to take into account is a threatening depletion of the non-renewable fossil fuels, in particular oil, a shortage of water, and the loss of farming soil by wind and water erosion. The latter might not seem that serious because only about one half of the Earth's arable land is currently used for farming. But further exploitation of this land will increase the loss of biodiversity, and it will also be relatively energy-consuming, since much of this land is less suitable for agriculture and more distant from densely populated areas. So, this exploitation will aggravate the threat of depletion of oil reserves. It is debateable how problematic this is, since the size of the oil reserves of the Earth are unknown, but many experts believe that oil production will peak in the imminent future, while consumption is likely to continue to increase steeply at least for a couple of decades.

All of these problems and others like them are 'collateral damage' of a technological advance, which has promoted a boost of the living standard and an explosion of the human population. In contrast to the problems considered in Chapter 4, they do not arise because of the malice or derangement of a smaller number of agents, but because of the selfish and short-sighted behaviour of masses of people. We shall be particularly concerned with these problems to the (considerable) extent that they are caused by the behaviour of the majority of citizens of affluent liberal democracies (though in the future they might to a greater extent be caused by developing countries because of their population growth and economical growth).

The type of case from which the problem of the tragedy of the commons derives its name is an environmental problem on a smaller scale. Suppose that if the herdsmen of a village let their cattle continue to graze to the current extent the pastures that they share, there will be overgrazing of them in the near future. As a consequence, the herdsmen will in the course of time be able to feed fewer cattle, and they and their families will eventually starve. Suppose further that if only a few herdsmen reduce the grazing of their cattle, and most of the other herdsmen do not do so, there will still be overgrazing, though it will occur somewhat later. Almost all of them will have to effect a reduction if overgrazing is to be avoided. Then it might not be rational for any individual herdsman to cut down on the grazing of his cattle. This will be rational only if he has good reason to believe that a sufficient number of the other herdsmen will do so as well, and especially if this number will not be sufficient without his own contribution. Thus, if trust in the willingness of fellow herdsmen to cooperate is faltering, there is a risk that each herdsman will let his cattle continue to graze as before, with the result that there is overgrazing and starvation for all in the future. There is a self-interested reason to reduce grazing only if this reduction is necessary to make up a number of reductions that is sufficient to prevent overgrazing. If there is doubt that there is a willingness to cooperate to this extent—or for that matter a belief that there is a willingness to cooperate beyond it—self-interest instead dictates defection from a cooperative endeavour.

Nonetheless, if the total number of the herdsmen is small enough, there could be a self-interested reason for each herdsman to opt for a reduction of the grazing of his cattle. If there is a chance that one herdsman's reduction is necessary for there to be a sum of reductions which is minimally sufficient to prevent overgrazing, there is an altruistic and utilitarian reason for him to cut down his grazing, since this will yield an outcome that is best for all. But as each herdsman is a member of the collective that is benefited, there is also something to be gained in terms of self-interest by cutting down.[1] Thus, as long as an individual herdsman's reduction makes a noticeable difference to the outcome, there may be a self-interested reason for him to make it because it is then possible that his reduction is necessary to produce, in conjunction with the other reductions in fact made, a set that is sufficient for the most beneficial outcome

---

[1] In contrast, it is not true in the prisoners' dilemma that there is also a self-interested reason to do what is best for all participants. This is true only if the dilemma is repeated without a foreseeable end, since if one then defects, tit-for-tat should lead one to expect that other parties who have tried to cooperate will be likely to punish one by excluding one from future cooperative ventures. But obviously, this is a reason which could kick in only if one expects future opportunities of cooperation with the same parties.

for a collective which includes the herdsman himself. All the same, the self-interested reason not to reduce grazing is normally greater for each and every herdsman, since the probability that his reduction will tip the scales is likely to be slim.

However, as the number of agents involved in the tragedy of common grows, we eventually reach a stage at which the reduction of grazing of each agent to the total outcome becomes negligible or imperceptible. Then an individual agent will have no altruistic or utilitarian reason and, a fortiori, no self-interested reason to reduce his grazing. This is because there is now no *determinate* threshold of reductions which makes them sufficient to prevent overgrazing. Moreover, if the number of agents involved is large, it also becomes harder to establish the trust necessary for cooperation because the individual agents are unlikely to know each other. So, it is unlikely that they will have developed concern and liking for each other. Likewise, it will be harder for them to keep an eye on each other and check whether there is free-riding. For all these reasons, the problem of the tragedy of the commons will be even harder to solve when the number of agents is so great that the contribution of each makes no appreciable difference to the total outcome.

It seems that what could make the individual herdsmen cooperate in these circumstances is only *a feeling of justice and fairness*; that it would be unfair to those who cut down on their grazing to free-ride on their sacrifices. We found in Chapter 2 that there is a ground for thinking that human beings are equipped with such a feeling of justice. If one believes that a sufficient number of other parties might make sacrifices, it would be unfair to them to be a free-rider taking advantage of their sacrifices without making any sacrifice oneself. But this feeling will be weaker when many of the other parties are anonymous to the individual agent, and the agent is likely to have no concern for them.

Imagine that in these circumstances, a sufficient number of herdsmen fail to cut down on the grazing of their cattle, so that there is overgrazing. Is each of them then responsible for the bad outcome, though it would have been as bad had he acted differently, since the damage he has caused was negligible? Yes, but this is not because the behaviour of each is a part of the cause of the outcome, without being causally necessary for it (as is true whenever there is causal overdetermination). Rather, it is because it is not necessary for every member of a collective that causes an outcome to make *any* individual causal contribution to the outcome in order for the member to be as morally responsible for the outcome as are those who do make a causal contribution.

To see that this is so, suppose there is a machine that will kill Vic if at least 51 out of a body of 100 voters vote in favour of execution. According to the procedure, all of the 100 voters must first give their votes. Then the machine starts counting them, and as soon as it has found 51 in favour of execution or release, it kills Vic or lets him go, in accordance with the vote of the majority. Now suppose that, say, 75 vote in favour of execution. This means that 24 votes in favour will not make *any* causal impact upon machine's killing; they are not even redundant parts of the cause of its killing. To ensure that this is the case, let us imagine that what votes the machine picks out is not determined by the order in which the votes are cast because the machine mixes the votes in a random way before it starts counting them. Consequently, the pro-death voters cannot influence the probability of their vote being among the ones that make the machine kill by voting early or late.

In these circumstances, the pro-death voters whose votes remain un-counted are surely as morally responsible as are those whose votes activated the machine's killing. All of the 75 pro-death voters are equally responsible in virtue of having cast their vote in favour of execution (assuming that they cast their votes intentionally and not mistakenly). Morally speaking, it makes no difference whether or not their votes happened to be among the 51 that were counted and, so, caused the machine to the kill Vic.[2] Therefore, even if some of the pro-death voters had correctly anticipated that their votes would remain uncounted, they could still cast their votes in order to be responsible for the execution by expressing their solidarity with those voters whose votes caused the machine to kill. They would then be responsible for the execution, even though they causally con-tributed as little to it as did those who voted against execution, and who are therefore not responsible for this outcome.[3]

---

[2] To be sure, the uncounted votes in favour of execution were part of the cause of the machine's starting to count, but so were the votes against execution.

[3] In contrast, Richard Tuck believes that even in cases in which more votes than are necessary are cast 'each vote carries the full causal responsibility for bringing about the result' (2008: 41). He argues, in opposition to counterfactual analyses of causation, that something could be (part of) a cause without being necessary for the effect. We are prepared to go along with this claim about causality—because we think it makes best sense of the phenomenon of overdetermination—but this does not imply that in the case at hand all of the pro-death voters are causally responsible for Vic's execution, since the 24 uncounted pro-death votes are

Likewise, all of the defecting herdsmen are equally morally responsible for the resulting overgrazing even if there is not a minimally sufficient number of reductions requisite to prevent it. From a moral point of view, it does not matter whether or not their defection was necessary to tip the scales in favour of overgrazing. If an individual act of defection was not necessary to tip the scales, this may be either because each defection made only a negligible difference, or because it made a non-negligible difference, which was not decisive because there was a sufficient number of defections independently of it. If each herdsman's defection made a noticeable difference, each of them could reasonably have had the belief that their own defection would be decisive if they had believed that most of them would go for reduction to stop overgrazing. They would then have had an altruistic or utilitarian reason to go along with the policy of reducing the grazing of their cattle. To repeat, this would also have provided them with a self-interested reason to cut down, though they would presumably have had a stronger self-interested reason not to do so, since it is improbable that their individual reduction would be required to tip the scales.

However, when the impact of the behaviour of each individual is negligible, there could be no such altruistic or utilitarian reason. The only reason to opt for reduction would then be a sense of the unfairness of free-riding if one is under the impression that a sufficient number of other parties will decide to cooperate. Yet, as the ultimatum games briefly considered in Chapter 2 show, people are sometimes willing to sacrifice benefits for the sake of considerations of fairness; so, the herdsmen could choose cooperation on the basis of this consideration. But if the impact of each party is negligible, since the number of parties involved is big and, consequently, the reluctance to be unfair to other parties tends to be weak because most of the parties will scarcely know each other, then the tragedy of the commons will be especially hard to void.

---

not even redundant parts of the cause of the execution. Quite simply, they are not causally operative. Nevertheless, on our view all of the pro-death voters could be equally and fully morally responsible for the execution, since our view separates moral responsibility from causal responsibility and, thus, from causation, and holds that one could be fully morally responsible for something without being even a redundant part of the cause of it. It is rather the intentions and beliefs that one has, or could be expected to have, when one acts that decide one's moral responsibility, i.e. the degree to which one is morally blame- or praiseworthy.

7

The Tragedy of the Environment and Liberal Democracy

The tragedy of the commons assumes such an acute form in the case of current anthropogenic climatic and environmental changes caused by large liberal democracies.[1] The citizens of these democracies are so numerous that the climatic and environmental effects of what they do together could be highly destructive, though the effects of each citizen's acts are negligible. Their number also makes it inevitable they are largely anonymous to each other. Thus, nobody has much of an altruistic or utilitarian reason to make any sacrifices. Trust and the feeling of having to be fair to fellow-citizens are on the whole thin, since most of them are strangers to each other. Also, their vast number makes it difficult for them to keep an eye on each other. Furthermore, what is needed is not just the cooperation of the present generation. It is useless for the present generation to make efforts to protect the climate and environment, unless it has reason to trust that the next generations will follow suit, and this assurance might well be hard to come by.

But while this is bad enough, there are further factors that make things even worse with respect to climatic and environmental issues. One such factor is that the causes and harmfulness to humans of climate change and its long-term environmental effects are to some extent debateable. It is controversial to what precise extent our emission of greenhouse gases affects the climate, e.g. what temperature increases will go with what

---

[1] This is argued at great length by Stephen Gardiner, 2011: chs. 4–6, but when Gardiner's book appeared, the present work was at a final stage, so it has not been influenced by Gardiner's analysis, in spite of there being parallels.

concentrations of carbon dioxide in the atmosphere. Nor is there a consensus about whether these climatic changes will be so great, or abrupt, that they would be seriously harmful to humans. Thus, it is a matter of some controversy as to what extent we are called upon to reduce our emission of greenhouse gases in order not to bring about a considerable deterioration of conditions of life on Earth in the future.

A different kind of complicating factor is that the worst climatic and environmental effects will occur in the distant future. As we have seen, people are prone to discount the distant future. Also, this temporal perspective leaves room for wishful thinking to the effect that in the future there will be novel technology to fix any damage done. Most human beings have a tendency to be too optimistic. This tendency manifests itself in the so-called planning fallacy—that humans think they can achieve more in the future than they have achieved in similar conditions in the past, for instance, that they will be able to stick to deadlines or resolutions to kick bad habits, although they have notoriously failed to do so in the past. Humans are prone to be too confident about their own capacities, e.g. almost all students who begin a course believe that they will end up in the top half at exams, almost all drivers believe that they are better than the average, and so on (see Dunning et al., 2004). Obviously, such a tendency could be more advantageous from the point of view of survival and reproduction of a group than a tendency to pessimism, which is likely to make one give up too easily. Even if many optimists were to fail in their overambitious goals, the success of some of them might be of decisive advantage to the group. In the eyes of this optimistic majority, those who have a more realistic view of their own abilities and the state of the world appear as pessimists. People suffering depression have been found to have a more accurate view of the world and themselves than people without depression. Healthy people tend to have inflated self images, positive illusions and view the world through 'rose coloured glasses' (see Alloy and Abramson, 1979, and Dobson and Franche, 1989).

A further contributing factor is that, while affluent nations, in particular the United States, are responsible for a disproportionate percentage of the world emission of greenhouse gases—1/5 in the case of the United States—the worst effects of global warming will probably be borne by people in other, poor countries, in Africa and South-East Asia (though the south-west of the US may be afflicted by droughts). As we have seen, we care less about foreigners. Cass Sunstein refers to 'a "revealed preference" study of American taxation and foreign aid/that/suggests that Americans value a non-American life in the poorer nations at 1/2,000 of the value they put on an American life' (2007: 46).

This lack of concern for the welfare of foreigners is surely part of the explanation of why developed countries have given so little aid to developing countries. The United States has spent roughly 3 trillion dollars in the last ten years on engaging in a 'war on terror' in Afghanistan and Iraq. In the last fifty years, it spent 2.1 trillion dollars on foreign aid. We should expect the United States to be at least as reluctant to make sacrifices of their quality of life to counteract an anthropogenic climate change that will have its worst consequences in far away countries. In fact, the US might even be *more* reluctant to make the latter sacrifices, since it will not only be distant strangers whom they will benefit, but strangers in a distant future. Two biases in human nature might unite forces here.

It might be objected that, while the misery that will result from anthropogenic climate change will have been caused in large part by people in wealthy nations, this is not so with the misery that foreign aid could alleviate. Therefore, according to our ingrained causally-based sense of responsibility, there will be a stronger sense of responsibility for the former misery and, thus, special obligations to prevent it. This argument is doubtful for several reasons. As we have already observed, it could well be true that the current poverty and social disorder of many developing countries to no small measure have been caused by Western democracies, in particular during their colonial past, but also today when they continue to exploit the natural resources of the developing world by unfair trade deals and by supporting corrupt governments. To be sure, these causal relations are contestable, but the same is likely to be true with respect to the undermining of future life conditions through anthropogenic climate change. The causal connections between these negative effects and the excessively consumerist lifestyle in Western democracies will be indirect and partly obscure. This is bound to dilute a causally-based sense of responsibility. Consequently, it seems likely that the reluctance of Western democracies to take steps to avoid causing harm in the developing world by means of climate change will be at least as strong as their current reluctance to aid the developing world.

However, there are some possible consequences of anthropogenic climate change that are harmful to Western democracies, e.g. countries like the Netherlands run a great risk of being inundated, and Australia runs a similar risk of severe droughts. There are also secondary effects of climate change that are detrimental to the interests of these democracies. For instance, if global warming brings along droughts and desertification in certain regions of the developing world, this could send gigantic waves of starving refugees to the gates of these democracies. It might be too blatantly inhumane to be politically feasible to keep the gates entirely closed, but if they are opened, it would put considerable pressure on the economy of these democracies as well as on their internal security for reasons detailed in Chapter 4.

To assess the probability of affluent people getting around to making the reductions of their consumption required to halt anthropogenic climatic change and environmental destruction, it is also necessary to consider how substantial these reductions would need to be. Affluent people need to find a level of consumption that is sustainable in the foreseeable future. This level is not the level that would be sustainable were the citizens of affluent democracies to maintain this level of consumption in the foreseeable future, on the assumption that the citizens of all other nations continue to consume *what they now do*. Clearly, global justice requires that affluent democracies find a level that would be sustainable even if hugely populous nations like China and India, which are on the rise economically, were to approach it. This sustainable welfare level will certainly be much lower than Western democracies now enjoy.

Even this requirement does not go far enough, however, for global justice requires these nations, which are affluent, or on their way to affluence, to seek a level which does not prevent poorer nations in the developing world from reaching the same level in the more remote future. (As we suggested in Chapter 5, they have even an obligation to assist developing countries to reach this level.) They need not strike a level that would be sustainable were all nations to attain it now or in the imminent future because that is not a realistic scenario. But they have to find a level that would be sustainable in the foreseeable future were all nations on Earth to attain it, or to approximate to it, in the foreseeable future. It would be grossly inhuman to aim for a level that does not leave enough natural resources for the worst off nations to come anywhere near the level of welfare that other countries enjoy.

This sustainable level of welfare is surely considerably lower than the current level in Western democracies. According to some estimates, if all of the 7 billion people alive today were to reach the living standard of people in Western democracies, the human impact upon the environment, in the form of consumption of resources and release of waste products would be twelve times higher than it is today (Diamond, 2005: 495). The impact upon the environment per capita of the billion people in the developed countries is thirty-two times as high as that of 5.5 billion people in the developing countries. This increase is evidently not sustainable, though we have left out of account the fact that the population on Earth is expected to continue to grow to 9 billion around 2050 and to 10 billion by the end of the century (according to the medium variant of the *2010 Revision of the World Population Prospects* by the United Nations). In 2004 roughly half of the world's population had to survive on less than 2 dollars a day, and 1.2 billion on less than 1 dollar. It is the population of these categories which will increase most, making an intolerable situation even worse.

Thus, consumption in affluent countries must be severely restrained to reach a sustainable level. This means that the individual liberty, which is a mark of these democracies, will have to be curtailed. Furthermore, this curtailment is likely to be felt as increasingly burdensome by the citizens of affluent democracies, since the consumption made possible by future technological advances is likely to continue to expand. In other words, an increasingly higher percentage of the technologically possible consumption will be out of bounds, morally speaking. We are used to picturing human history as a story of progress; never before have so many people led lives of such a high standard as today. On the other hand, it is also true that never before have so many people lived in abject poverty and misery. But we who are fortunate tend to suppress this fact and to represent human history as an unqualified success story in which the development of scientific technology takes us to ever new heights. However, if citizens of the affluent liberal democracies were to make the cutbacks that are necessary to attain sustainability, their future will not be a new all-time high. It would instead be an unpleasant step down from the unrestrained consumerism of the past.

Examples of restrictions that will be felt in everyday life include the following. The consumption of meat, especially red meat, will need to be abandoned or reduced in favour of vegetarian food in order to decrease the percentage of land used for raising animals—now 80 per cent of the land used for food production—and to decrease the release of methane from ruminating cattle, which contributes to global warming. Furthermore, a change to a vegetarian diet will mean that the quantity of water necessary to produce human food is cut down to half of what it is now, and water shortage is another problem that the world faces. A shift to a vegetarian diet will also reduce the risk of pandemics, which are prone to arise where there are high concentrations of domestic animals in close contact with large human populations, as in the Guandong province of China.

As regards transport, there will need to be restrictions on car and air travel because, by the emission of carbon dioxide, they contribute to climate change. According to some new studies, if the emission of carbon dioxide continues at the present rate—though, as remarked, it is likely to increase because of the economic growth of populous nations like China, India and Brazil—we shall by 2030 reach a level which causes a temperature rise by $2°C$, a rise that is regarded by politicians to be the limit of what is acceptable. Also, we might be short of oil in a few decades, which is worrying because of our huge and increasing dependence upon it. Restrictions like the ones mentioned will be felt as severe restrictions of the liberty and freedom of citizens in democracies, as well as a significant loss of well-being.

A further possible restriction could be on reproduction: since the world is already overpopulated, a plausible case could be made for restricting the number of children to at most two per woman. The UN *Universal Declaration of Human Rights*, 1948, article 16 states that 'Men and women of full age . . . have the right to marry and to found a family'—without putting any limit upon the size of the family. In an overpopulated world, this seems an irresponsible policy. It might be objected that a restriction on reproduction in affluent countries is superfluous, since the average birth rate is already lower than two children per woman in many of these countries. But it should be observed that the 'carbon legacy' of one US child—i.e. the carbon emissions that it and its descendants are expected to be responsible for—is 130 times greater than that of a child from Bangladesh and 50 times higher than that of an Indian child (Hamilton, 2010: 43). Furthermore, in some affluent countries efforts are made to increase birth rate, e.g. by governmental subsidies, out of fear that the future workforce might otherwise be too small to support a growing number of pensioners. This ignores that the demands of work force could be filled by immigrants. So, we think that these countries should contemplate keeping birth rates down by removing subsidies for children, except for the first two, and perhaps imposing taxes on additional children. This could be done without denying that it is the high birth rate in the developing countries that creates the major humanitarian problem.

Such restrictions are justifiable independently of the issue of the extent to which people in affluent countries ought to aid people in the developing world to attain a decent and sustainable standard of living. If the inhabitants of affluent countries have obligations to this effect, which, for reasons indicated in Chapter 5, seems credible, the reduction of their standard of living will of course be even more extensive, though it is debatable how much more extensive it will be. But it will be demanding enough if the reduction is to be sufficient not to *prevent* these poor nations from arriving at the same level, or even if the reduction is to be compatible with giant nations on the economic rise, such as China, India, and Brazil, arriving at it. If China alone were to reach this level, the present human impact upon the environment is estimated to double (Diamond, 2005: 495).

It seems unlikely that the citizens of Western democracies will voluntarily consent to such harsh restraints. In support of this conjecture, consider that 52 per cent of US citizens have declared that they would refuse to support the Kyoto Protocol if it would cost an average household an extra 50 dollars per month, and only 11 per cent would support it if the cost rose to 100 dollars or more (Sunstein, 2007: 44). A survey in Sweden at the end of 2010 shows that the extent to which its citizens eat meat, drive cars, and fly has increased rather than decreased in the four years since the publication of Al Gore's *An Inconvenient Truth* caused a stir—in spite of the economic recession of world economy.

These facts indicate that merely informing citizens about the consequences of their resource-consuming lifestyle will probably not suffice.[2] This is not just because the citizens will have to sacrifice a lot of comfort and entertainment to which they have grown accustomed, which is something that most people would be loath to do. It is also because these sacrifices will be useless, and will have no appreciable effect upon

---

[2] It should not be denied that making information about environmental impact more accessible could take us part of the way. In their much discussed book, Thaler and Sunstein describe how various 'nudges' could improve our conduct (2009: ch. 12). But since nudges, by definition, 'must be easy and cheap to avoid' (2009: 6), they are not well suited to induce behavioural changes that should be radical and permanent. They are better suited to make us overcome backsliding on isolated occasions, to make us execute what we already think is best for us, or to make us decide between roughly equally balanced alternatives. To give just one example, nudges on packs of cigarettes are unlikely to suffice to make smokers quit for good.

the climate and environment unless a sufficient number of other individuals follow suit. In contemporary societies with populations so large that most citizens are anonymous to each other, the only way to provide a basis for such assurance is presumably by their governments imposing regulations and penalizing those who do not respect them. For instance, they could introduce a far-reaching cap-and-trade system in which those who pollute have to buy permissions to a certain amount of pollution and these permissions are traded in a market. Or they could put heavy taxes on the consumption of certain resources, for instance, taxes either on the acquisition of fossil fuels, or on emissions from them. Such taxes will not merely decrease the use of these fuels directly; they will also stimulate research into cleaner energy, like sun, wind, and hydrogen energy, and more effective methods of carbon sequestration. In the absence of such regulations sanctioned by all or most governments, it seems overwhelmingly likely that most citizens and companies of affluent democracies will continue their disastrous over-exploitation of natural resources.

However, governments in liberal democracies are likely to be disinclined to propose such regulations. Apart from the fact that their political leaders will privately suffer from a resulting welfare squeeze, proposals to this effect also appear suicidal from the point of view of their career. Such proposals are prone to make politicians unpopular and likely to lose the next election if there are competing parties that advocate more generous policies. And there will surely be such competitors because generosity towards the voters appears to be a foolproof way of gaining power if rival political parties propose tougher restrictions. Also, political parties favouring status quo will be subsidized by vested interests in fossil fuels and other currently lucrative products. By contrast, politicians run a definite career risk by taking a lenient attitude towards the possibility of terrorist attacks, since if there happen to be any major terrorist attacks in the near future, their re-election will be jeopardized. But as climatic and environmental changes are slow working, they will not have time to build up to calamitous magnitudes before the responsible politicians are long since out of office, and even dead (Sunstein, 2007: 47–8). Related to this is the fact that in order to be effective, sustainable policies would need to be adhered to for decades. This means that it would be senseless for politicians to introduce them now, and put their careers at risk, unless they can trust that the next generations of leaders stick to them. A ground for such a trust might well be hard to muster. So, democratic leaders have much to gain and little, if anything, to lose by underestimating the need to mitigate anthropogenic climatic change and environmental destruction.

This political evasiveness is facilitated by the fact that evidence of harmful climate change is unlikely to be incontestable in the imminent future, since climate change is creeping in on us gradually. For instance, glacial melting from one year to another is unnoticeable; one needs to look back several decades to be struck by its extent. There is a natural variation of temperatures from one year to another, which can mask an underlying trend of rising temperature. It is tempting to deny or downplay ominous signs when acknowledging them would make great sacrifices incumbent upon us, and their unobtrusiveness in this case makes it particularly easy to do so. As already remarked, politicians in democracies appear to be especially prone to do so, since they can put off unpopular cutbacks without risking any personal reprisals.

Even when harmful climatic changes are undeniable, it will still be disputable to what precise extent they are anthropogenic, caused by human activities. After all, the Earth underwent remarkable climate changes long before humans appeared on the scene. But the hitch is that when our detrimental effect upon the climate and the environment of the planet becomes undeniable, it might be impossible for us to reverse the process of degradation. This is because greenhouse gases remain in the atmosphere for a long time, making further temperature increases inescapable. Rainforests which absorb carbon dioxide will dry out; Arctic and Antarctic ice covers will melt and the albedo effect will decrease; permafrost regions in Siberia will also thaw, releasing large quantities of methane. As a result, the temperature increase will be stoked up, even if all human emissions of greenhouse gases were to cease. Nevertheless, conservative political parties, and lobby groups supporting them, are prone to exploit any uncertainty there is about harmful anthropogenic climate change to win the day. When there is no longer any uncertainty to be exploited, it might be too late to reverse the decline effectively. In this respect, waiting for a climatic or environmental disaster before taking action is more fateful than waiting for a major act of terrorism. We cannot expect that there will be an environmental and climatic 9/11 that will make us wake up in time to prevent even bigger disasters.

The tragedy of the commons will be in operation not only in domestic politics, but also in foreign affairs. Politicians in democracies will probably be disinclined to propose welfare cutbacks in their own countries that risk removing them from power if they have no assurance that such policies will be implemented in so many other states all over the world that the effect upon the global climate will be sufficient. Such assurance could be forthcoming only if reliable, world-wide agreements are in place, but this seems out of reach. For instance, neither the UN climate meeting in Copenhagen 2009, nor the one in Cancún 2010, resulted in any binding restrictions on the emission of greenhouse gases that could replace the Kyoto Protocol of 1997, which lapses in 2012. A chief reason for this failure is the huge global inequality in respect of economy and welfare. The Kyoto Protocol proposed no restrictions on the emission of greenhouse gases by populous nations like China and India. It is not surprising that there were no such restrictions, since it is not easy to think of regulations that would be acceptable to both the United States, on the one hand, and China and India, on the other.

A sustainable rate of emissions, which is proportionate to the population of a nation, would scarcely be acceptable to the US, as it would realistically mean a massive reduction of the current level of its emissions. China has just bypassed the US as having the biggest total of emissions of carbon dioxide, but the per capita emission in China is one fifth of the one in the US, which is one of the highest in the world. Together these nations are responsible for around 40 per cent of the world's emissions. A sustainable rate which is proportionate to the size of population would mean at least an 80 per cent reduction for the US, which is surely politically impossible. However, a more modest reduction of the emissions of the US would put China and India in a position to claim rights to much larger total emissions, in view of their much larger populations, and in view of the fact that they have hitherto contributed relatively little to the greenhouse effect. The developed nations have been responsible for 75 per cent of the greenhouse gases that have been put in the atmosphere since 1850: the US has been responsible for 29 per cent and the countries of EU for 26 per cent, while China and India have only been responsible for 8 per cent and 2 per cent respectively.[3] So, the suggestion that developed nations with big per capita emissions and a bad historical record need only make modest reductions would pave the way for claims from countries like China and India to emission rights that are far too permissive from an environmental

---

[3] On the other hand, the developing nations are expected to be responsible for 90 per cent of the rise of emissions during the next century (Hamilton, 2010: 5).

perspective. This is obvious, since a reduction of emissions that would be acceptable to the US is likely to have to be *very* modest. It is especially unlikely that the US government would accept any significant cuts as the US is less exposed to the detrimental effects of climate change than are many other countries, and the parochial altruism of humans makes them rather unconcerned about their fellow-beings in other parts of the world.

So far we have talked about economic obstacles to international agreements, but we must not forget that ideological and religious differences could also be major stumbling blocks. It is a familiar sociological fact that such differences buttress distrust and isolation, both within and between societies. Ideological and religious clashes have been responsible for a great deal of the inefficiency of the UN since the end of the Second World War. Some of these clashes have become significantly less intense—e.g. those between capitalism and communism, which were called the Cold War—but they have been replaced by others, in particular the polarization between the West and the Islamic sphere. Religion is involved in the most recalcitrant and long-standing conflicts in the world today, like the conflict between Israel and Palestine and between India and Pakistan.

All in all, it seems that affluent democracies will find it very hard to establish a consistent, long-term conservation policy which could prevent a threatening climatic and environmental crisis. Democratic politicians are badly suited to implement such a policy because they have to please the majority of their citizens who look bent upon deriving as much satisfaction as possible out of the advances of science. But the consumptive desires of the majority seems bound to deplete the resources of the Earth when the majority amounts to billions, and science has put into its possession the means of an excessively extensive exploitation of nature.

A study of history seems to indicate that the rise of liberal democracy was nurtured by the industrialization and the increase of the general standard of living that followed in its wake. Liberal democracy began to emerge in Europe roughly at the same time as industrialization did, some 200 years ago. It is reasonable to think that when the standard of living of citizens went up, they became well nourished and well educated enough to demand more political power. Democracy offers this in the shape of an equal right to vote. It will be interesting to see if this democratization process will repeat itself in the economically successful China, or whether its economic success will rather nourish a nationalistic pride that will make it emphasize its own more authoritarian traditions. The fact that success of China is coming at a time when Western democracies show clear signs of failing to deal with their financial crises may make the latter alternative more probable.

Anthropogenic climate change and environmental degradation are probably the greatest challenges to liberal democracy so far because an arrest or marked mitigation of them requires that the majority in affluent democracies sacrifice their self-interest to promote the interests of future generations, including future generations of people in faraway countries, and non-human animals. This restraint of self-interest is the very opposite of the unrestrained satisfaction of it made possible by industrialization and its profusion of material goods, which brought liberal democracy into existence. Liberal democracy has so far been a politics of prosperity, and this induces doubt whether it could turn into a politics of parsimony, voluntary restraint, and decreasing welfare. One might be especially pessimistic about the prospects of halting the loss of biodiversity, since it seems almost inevitable that the interests of other species will have to take the back seat in the increasingly sharp clashes with human interests. But there is a fact that could keep alive a glimmer of hope: thirty-four regions covering just 2.3 per cent of the Earth's surface contain 75 per cent of the most threatened mammals, birds, and amphibians (Martin, 2006: 388). Surely, it should not require superhuman efforts to protect these last remaining vestiges of biodiversity.

Things to which we have been accustomed for a long time exercise a strong hold upon our imagination—this is the availability basis. For instance, although we all know that we shall eventually die, we find it difficult, as long as we are well, to imagine vividly the situation of being about to die because we are so used to being alive and well. Analogously, we are so used to our comfortable way of living that we find it hard to imagine that our descendents could one day be deprived of it because of our destructive influence on the climate and environment. During the course of human history more and more people have enjoyed better and longer lives. Most of us are inclined to take it for granted that this development will go on, according to the same pattern, and that it is unnecessary for us now to undertake protective measures, since future generations will be so much better equipped to do so, thanks to scientific progress. But this way of thinking fails to take seriously the fact that the climatic and environmental problems will also be graver in the future for reasons that we have already detailed. Because climate change and environmental destruction sneak up on us, we might not realize the danger of them until we have reached a tipping point at which further deterioration is irreversible. As already noted, there is in this respect a contrast to the threat of terrorism, where the risk is instead a public overreaction because indisputable instances of terrorist attacks, like 9/11, starkly illustrate how horrifying they can be.

8

Authoritarianism and Democracy

Non-democratic, authoritarian forms of government are better placed than democracies to implement unpopular reforms effectively. This is increasingly so the more robust or securely in power the authoritarian governments are. Whether this greater efficiency is a good or bad thing depends upon whether the unpopular reforms are overall beneficial or harmful. Since it is to be feared that unpopular policies of authoritarian regimes most often promote the interests of the ruling elite, serve to consolidate its power or to enrich it, rather than promoting the interests of the citizens, a strong argument in favour of democracy is that it provides an opportunity to get rid of unpopular leaders without the use of violence, by regular general elections. States which are formally democratic may not in reality live up to this ideal e.g. because their citizens are indoctrinated or coerced by the leaders to vote for more or less whatever they propose. But if states do live up to this ideal and are what one might call paradigmatic democracies, it will be harder for leaders in them to implement generally unpopular policies than for leaders in robustly authoritarian states. To repeat, this is probably in most cases a virtue, since most unpopular policies seem in fact to have been bad ones, but it may in some cases be a drawback.[1]

As a possible illustration of a beneficial unpopular reform, consider the one-child policy that China enforced in 1979. This coercive policy has been criticized by appeal to the UN *Universal Declaration of Human Rights*,

---

[1] Since we are stressing the difficulties that democracies face in coping with climatic and environmental problems, we should note that, on the other hand, democracies have been largely successful in avoiding some other very harmful policies, like genocide and aggressive wars (Pinker, 2011: 278–84, 320–43), which have often issued from authoritarian regimes.

1948, article 16, which we have already quoted. Against this background, it is not surprising that the more democratic country of India was not successful in applying coercive means like the ones employed by China. Indira Gandhi's government attempted a coercive vasectomy policy in the 1970s, but lost the next election, in 1977. Subsequently, the issue was dropped in India, and the upshot is that, although in 1995 the population of China was 1.2 billion and of India 900 million, in 2020 the population of both countries is expected to be the same, somewhere between 1.3 and 1.4 billion. It is expected that this level is where it will peak in China, whereas in India it will continue to increase to 1.7 billion in 2070. Not surprisingly, the standard of living in India is now lagging behind that in China.

It is not unreasonable to think that it would have been advantageous, both nationally and internationally, if India had introduced a policy similar to that of China. This is so, although largest population growth is predicted to occur in Africa where there is predicted to be an increase from 1 billion to 3.6 billion at the end of the century (according to the *2010 Revision of the World Population Prospects*). These are the poorest countries on Earth, and if the people in them are to attain anything like a decent standard of living, it will put an enormous strain on the resources of the planet. As already noted, if there were only the seven billion people who inhabit this planet today, and they were to attain the current living standard of people in Western democracies, the human impact upon the environment would be twelve times higher than what it now is. Needless to say, it would be grossly immoral to hope that this catastrophic impact is avoided by a considerable portion of the Earth's population continuing to live in abject poverty.

It is an established fact that there is a correlation between the levelling off of population growth and a boost of the standard of living (see e.g. Seitz, 2008: ch. 2, for a brief summary of the facts and references). The full explanation of this correlation is complex, but one part of it is certainly that as the standard of living rises, effective contraceptive technology and knowledge of birth control are likely to be available. Indeed, family planning programmes are so effective in reducing the birth rate that they have been found to work even in the absence of economic growth (Seitz, 2008: 59). Still, future population growth is expected to be largest in the poorest countries. Suppose that we divide the nations of the world into the three categories: affluent nations, developing nations, and destitute nations.[2] At present the first and the last category contain roughly a billion people each. It seems likely that in the next couple of decades these categories will increase to contain two billion each, the first by the standard of living rising for many in the second category, e.g. many people in China and India, the third because population growth is largest in this group. But if that is so, the human impact upon the environment will increase chiefly for two reasons: that the living standard rises in the second category of developing countries, and that population growth continues to be especially strong in the third category of destitute nations, but also in some of the poorer developing countries.

We have no reason, then, to expect that the environmental problems created by humans will be solved, unless resolute action is taken to this effect. But such action is likely to be widely unpopular, and it will have to be quick—quick enough to occur within the next couple of decades or so—to stop the progressive deterioration of the global climate and environment before it becomes irreversible. We have suggested that democracies will be hard put to implement such actions.

By contrast, dictatorships could rapidly bring about unpopular changes of lifestyle. As remarked, China, not being a democracy, is thereby at an advantage as regards an effective implementation of environmental-friendly policies. During Mao Zedong's regime, China, like the Soviet Union under Stalin, rapidly went through an industrialization process which had taken centuries in Europe. Could China equally rapidly neutralize the bad effects of this process? It phased out lead in petrol much more swiftly than did the West. It seems most likely, however, that as long as the living standard in Western democracies remains as high as it is, China will as a matter of national pride aim for the same level. This is corroborated by such facts as that the Chinese government is currently subsidizing petrol so heavily that car owners can buy it at a price *lower* than the market price. Furthermore, Chinese authorities might put their power at peril if they were to sanction policies that put short-term welfare increase second to longer-term environmental concerns. There is no reason to believe that public awareness of environmental problems is higher in China than in the West. Still, because the authoritarianism of the Chinese government seems rather robust, it would be less surprising if it made a sudden turnaround to

---

[2] As James Martin notes, many of the so-called developing countries are really destitute countries sinking deeper into destitution (2006: 110).

a greener and cleaner lifestyle than if the US succeeded in so doing. In the US the climate change debate has become increasingly politically coloured: in 1997, 52 per cent of Democrat voters and 48 per cent of Republican voters believed in anthropogenic climate change, but in 2008 this small difference of 4 per cent had grown to a difference of 34 per cent, with 76 per cent of Democrat voters and 42 per cent Republican voters having this belief (Hamilton, 2010: 108). This tendency is likely to hamper the pursuit in the US of a consistent climate policy in the longer term, since the political power is liable to pass between Democrat and Republican hands.

It should be added, however, that authoritarian regimes are usually at a disadvantage epistemically: relevant scientific research and findings are often suppressed for ideological reasons (another example of effective implementation of policies). For instance, there is reason to believe that the authoritarian nature of Chinese government prevented early action from being taken on avian flu. However, if the relevant climatic and environmental facts are already widely known, a general epistemic disadvantage of authoritarianism might not be crucial with respect to this issue. But, in any case, we are not arguing that, all things considered, the authoritarian regime of China is in a better position than Western democracies to get effective environmental-friendly policies going.

Theoretically, a meritocracy consisting of a scientifically educated elite with authoritarian power could sufficiently quickly install environmental-friendly policies. However, for reasons presented in Chapter 7, it is most improbable that such a meritocracy will be established by democratic elections, and even if it were, this would be irrelevant to the present topic, which is whether liberal democracies could handle anthropogenic climate change and other environmental problems, without ceasing to be liberal democracies.

David Shearman and Joseph Wayne Smith contend, as we have done, that liberal democracy will find it difficult to cope with environmental problems due to the tragedy of commons writ large (2007: 83). In their opinion, democracy will give way to some sort of authoritarian regime. Their main reason for thinking that this will happen is that authoritarianism has a 'biological basis' (2007: 99). According to their view, the most important political problem is therefore that of selecting 'the right sort of elites' to rule us (2007: 90). In essence they accept Plato's recipe for this selection (2007: ch. 9). We are inclined to think that this problem of selection of a reliable ruling elite is insoluble and, consequently that meritocracy is no viable way out. Even if some are better qualified than others to be political leaders, there is bound to be an endless disagreement about who these people are, a disagreement which might easily lead to the use of violence. And as long as the public do not accept that anyone is fit to govern them, they have no legitimate authority to do so.

Our question, then, is not whether it would be best if some form of authoritarianism were to replace present-day liberal democracy. We are assuming that it is best to retain democracy, and asking how it could overcome the mega threats currently facing humanity. In Chapter 4, we suggested that liberal democracy will probably have to become less liberal in response to the possibility of terrorists with weapons of mass destruction. In the last chapters we have been discussing the apparently even greater difficulty it will have to implement welfare-shrinking sustainable policies because their pay-offs lie in the remote future. The solution we shall tentatively propose is not abandonment of the democracy, but enhancement of the morality of its voters.

9

Liberal Democracy and the End of History

In 1992, Francis Fukuyama published a widely discussed book, *The End of History and the Last Man*, in which he suggested that history could come to an 'end' with liberal democracy: 'we can argue that history has come to an end if the present form of social and political organization/i.e. liberal democracy/is *completely satisfying* to human beings in their most essential characteristics' (1992: 136). At the time when Fukuyama wrote his book, a wave of democratization swept across the world. The Berlin Wall fell, and the Soviet Union dissolved into a number of independent states, at least some of which could lay claim to being liberal democracies. Consequently, at that time it might have seemed reasonable to be optimistic about the prospects of a world-wide democratization process. But this process appears to have been halted by the resurgence of Islamic fundamentalism and nationalism. We shall not attempt to predict whether this halt is temporary, and liberal democracy will resume its geographical expansion. We are, however, sceptical of the idea that history as a process of social and political development has an 'end', or a point at which it will come to rest because the current social and political order is 'completely satisfying', and there is nothing to stimulate further development or change. This is so regardless of whether this end be thought to be democracy or some other form of government.

According to Fukuyama, liberal democracy satisfies our material needs by being well suited to a high degree of scientific and technological development which, with a free market, promotes a high material standard of living. It also satisfies our social need for recognition by giving equal recognition to all citizens, rather than more recognition to some (the rulers) at the expense of others (the subjects). Fukuyama grants that liberal democracy does not perfectly gratify the craving for recognition—after all, we want to be recognized as superior rather than merely as equal to others—and conjectures that this is the chief threat to the hegemony of democracy (1992: 314). But he nevertheless believes that liberal democracy better than any other form of government gratifies the craving for recognition.

As regards the fulfilment of our material needs, Fukuyama writes: 'Technology makes possible the limitless accumulation of wealth, and thus the satisfaction of an ever-expanding set of human desires' (1992: p. xiv). He observes that this gives rise to problems of 'environmental damage and the frivolity of consumerism' (1992: p. xiv), but believes that 'these problems are not obviously insoluble on the basis of liberal principles, nor so serious that they would necessarily lead to the collapse of society as a whole' (1992: p. xxi). Today this should seem overly optimistic to most of us. We have argued that climatic and environmental problems stem from the very heart of democracy—the behaviour of the majority. It would seem unrealistic to believe that, in the few decades that remain before the climate and the environment are irreparably destroyed, the majority could direct itself onto a radically different path than the path of consumerism that it is hitherto followed. If this pessimism is well grounded, the very same process of technological progress and industrialization that, among others, Fukuyama believes (1992: ch. 10) to have paved the road for liberal democracy might bring about its downfall. It might be feared that liberal democracies will contribute to the depletion of natural resources to the extent that conflicts with weapons of mass destruction over dwindling natural resources will be provoked. That is to say, liberal democracy might be instrumental in bringing about the end of human history in a much more tragic sense than the one that Fukuyama had in mind.

To our minds it seems that human beings—in particular, males—are competitive and desire to surpass their fellow-beings in respect of not only recognition, but also in respect of material possessions because this provides reproductive advantages. A political order that gives equal recognition to all could not provide much satisfaction to the human desire for recognition because, as Thomas Hobbes put it in *De Cive* more than 350 years ago, recognition or glory 'is nothing if everybody has it, since it consists in comparison and preeminence' (1651: I. ii). Therefore, the craving for recognition appears destined to issue in conflicts between citizens, and any compromises are liable to be short-lived and to break down as relations of strength or liaisons change.

It might seem that this competitiveness of human nature will not necessarily destabilize liberal democracies for the reason that they give equal recognition to all citizens only in a rather formal way, by bestowing upon all of them certain basic civil rights and liberties. As we have already indicated, there is room for considerable socio-economic inequality in democracies, and the better off are likely to receive more recognition than the worse off, and their wealth will enable them to make better use of their rights and liberties. Furthermore, there are political inequalities: those who are elected to offices receive much more recognition. This creates a problem because one might doubt that political representatives who are so much more privileged than most of their voters could imaginatively put themselves in the shoes of the latter. For instance, it is hard to imagine that members of the US Congress who earn around 170, 000 dollars annually could put themselves in the shoes of the 15 per cent of the US citizens who live in poverty.[1]

This socio-economic inequality which provides an outlet for the struggle for recognition—a seemingly ineradicable trait of (at least male) human nature—also gives rise to a social divisiveness and distrust, which could destabilize a democracy. It has been suggested, e.g. by Fukuyama (1992: ch. 20), that democracy has been stable only in countries which, apart from exhibiting a fair amount of socio-economic equality, have been held together by strong cultural bonds, such as a sturdy sense of nationalism or a common religion. Even if this is going too far,[2] it would seem that the current form of the increasing multiculturalism of liberal democracies, with ingredients from cultures with authoritarian and theocratic rather than democratic traditions, presents a threat to their political system. A multicultural society in which people belonging to different ethnic groups live together is a sympathetic vision, but it has to grapple with the latent xenophobia of humankind. It appears that ethnic differences tend to breed distrust (Putnam, 2007). In the course of time the cultural diversity of a multicultural society might seem bound to decrease because the different constituent cultures will to some degree blend (for advocates of multiculturalism who are wont to cherish cultural diversity this will be

---

[1] This is one reason why some would claim that these democracies are not real democracies, but then one might wonder whether real democracies could ever materialize.

[2] After all, democracy seems strong in some culturally diversified countries, e.g. Belgium, Canada, Switzerland, and the US.

an unwelcome effect). Multiculturalism is also likely to obliterate racial differences due to interbreeding. This reduction of cultural and genetic differences might in the longer run weaken the foothold of xenophobia. However, this homogenization process might not have sufficient time to take effect. We observed in Chapter 4 that the multiculturalism of liberal democracies risks making them havens for ethnic groups that oppose its ideals and are ready to resort to violence to further their cause. Increased access to nuclear, biological, and chemical weapons of mass destruction might enable them to do this very effectively. The fear and anger aroused by such threats of terrorism could make xenophobia flare up and cause the formation of various racist and nationalist parties which violently confront the ethnic groups associated with these activities.[3] For this reason liberal democracies might be destabilized before the homogenization trend has achieved any significant results.

The root of this problem of stability is in the ideology of liberalism. According to liberalism, the state should strive for ideological neutrality; that is why liberalism insists upon, for instance, a divide between state and religion. If pushed to the extreme, the liberal ideal of neutrality becomes paradoxical, since it is itself an ideological stance which entails, e.g. that all human beings (and no non-human animals) are equals and have the same rights.[4] Nevertheless, this—imperfect—neutrality provides a lot of leeway for other ideologies, so ideologies at odds with liberal democracy could come forth and undercut its hegemony. We do not want to predict how likely this is, but only point out that this is a possibility that should be taken seriously. It is true that it has rarely happened that democracy has given way to authoritarianism, but it has happened, perhaps most notoriously when German democracy gave way to Nazi authoritarianism, with disastrous results. Our point is that the possibility of such developments is so much more serious today because of the existence of weapons of mass destruction, which could cause Ultimate Harm.

---

[3] For instance, as we were finishing this book, Anders Behring Breivik killed 77 people in Oslo and surroundings in a sort of one-man crusade against a leading political party allegedly too favourable towards multiculturalism and Muslim immigration in Norway.

[4] Against the backdrop of the avowed religious neutrality, it is awkward that the historical background of the doctrine of equal human rights appears to be the Judeo-Christian religious tradition (see e.g. Veatch, 1986, and Waldron, 2002), and that this doctrine is hard to justify without this religious underpinning.

However, even if the hegemony of liberal democracy is not stable and will not last, liberal democracy could still be the best or ideal form of government. At first blush, it might seem natural to go along with Plato and claim that it is best if those who are best qualified to rule do rule, i.e. that the ideal form of government is a meritocratic or epistocratic one. But, as already remarked, there is likely to be more or less as much informed and qualified disagreement about whom these political experts are as about what the right political decisions are. And as long as nobody is recognized as fit to lead by those who are to be led, nobody has any legitimate authority to lead, even if in fact they happen to be the best leaders.

A fair resolution of such disagreements would be to give everyone who is informed or qualified an equal say about what the right political decisions should be, or about who should rule. This is something that the majority rule of democracy does, but it is not the only decision procedure that would be fair: a fair lottery among the political proposals presented would also resolve matters without favouring anyone. Imagine that after a free, wide-ranging, public discussion, a decision is made, not by a majority vote, but by a fair lottery between the proposals thrown up. Why is the former procedure to be preferred to the latter if both are fair? Two possible replies would be: (a) more citizens will be guaranteed to be satisfied with political decisions if they are the outcome of a majority rule, and (b) the decisions will be wiser and morally better because the majority is a better guide to truth than the randomness of a lottery.[5] The first condition is subordinate to the second because if a political decision is grossly unfair and discriminatory to some minority, it might be morally unjustifiable though it satisfies the majority.

That a majority decision is grossly unfair to a minority is least likely to happen in a small community in which everyone knows everyone else, and there is mutual concern and trust. A small community is also liable to be less ethnically diverse. Democratic decisions would probably be most likely to be morally correct in such small communities with a primitive technology, which does not generate a large enough amount of welfare to make possible a significant economic inequality, and which does not have a far-reaching impact upon surrounding societies and the future. The

---

[5] That it is not enough that democracy represents a form of government that is fair, but that its decisions must also possess some epistemic virtue in the sense of being more likely to be right than a random procedure is forcefully argued by David Estlund, 2008.

political decisions in such communities will be much simpler and will concern only matters 'close to home'; the situation of the voters and their families. The more the consequences of the political decisions of a community extend beyond the community itself and its immediate future, the less strong the case for the soundness of its majority decisions becomes. For then they will affect individuals who have not taken part in the decision making, and parochial altruism, the bias towards the near future and the numbness to large numbers of those who have taken part will mean that individuals who have not taken part are at risk of being harmed through want of concern. Thus, we have reason to believe that the political decisions of contemporary liberal democracies will often be morally wrong because of these motivational shortcomings of people. To this should be added that these decisions might also be wrong because voters in general lack sufficient scientific knowledge to understand the relevant issues; it takes quite a bit of knowledge of various scientific disciplines to get a grip on how the lifestyle of current liberal democracies could affect the future of the planet.

Let us turn now to the issue of whether majority decisions have a better chance of being correct than decisions by a fair lottery. In democratic theory, attempts have been made to gain mileage out of the so-called *jury theorem*. Suppose that, when voting about two alternatives, each voter is slightly more likely to be right than a random process, say, to be right 51 per cent of the time. Then, the theorem declares that, if the number of voters is huge, it is virtually certain that the majority of them will come down in favour of the right alternative. This is as obvious as it is that, if we weight a huge number of coins such that there is a 51 per cent probability that they will show heads if they are flipped, then, if we flip them all, it is virtually certain that at least 51 per cent of them will show heads. All this might sound reassuring, though it should be borne in mind that in actual political life it is frequently hard to specify what the relevant alternatives are, and in any case they are certainly most often more than two. Also, the right alternative might not be on the table. We spoke above of the alternatives thrown up in a free, public debate. But, as we have earlier remarked, in democracies there is a market economy, which has normally created a great economic inequality. By controlling the mass media, strong business interests could ensure that the morally right alternative is unlikely to come up for discussion, or that it will come up only in a distorted form. If it comes up in a distorted form, each voter might be slightly *less* likely than a random process to be right and then, according to the jury theorem, the majority will almost certainly be wrong! This will also be the case if people are slightly less likely to be right than wrong because they are biased in some of the ways that we have described.

Against the idea, proposed most famously by J. S. Mill (1861), that certain classes of a society, the educated classes, should be endowed with votes of greater weight—the reason being that they are likely to have a more thorough understanding of political issues—it has been urged that this might favour the interests of these classes at the expense of the interests of other classes of the society (Estlund, 2008: ch. 11). For we are likely to be more or less partial in our own favour, even though we try to be impartial. This argument no doubt has a point. But, as is often enough noted, even if all adult citizens of a society have votes of the same weight, the majority rule by itself cannot guarantee that minorities are not discriminated against. The bigger a society is, the more likely it is that it will be ethnically diverse, and the more ethnically diverse, the greater the risk that some ethnic minority will be discriminated against, because people are naturally prone to xenophobia or discrimination against 'out-groups'. For this reason many actual democracies have constitutional constraints to protect minorities.

On the other hand, if a democracy becomes very extensive, there will be fewer outsiders who could be affected by its decisions, without having a vote. If a global democracy were established, the number of such outsiders would be minimized. Since the world-wide cooperation that is probably necessary to mitigate climate change could then be legally sanctioned, the establishment of a global democracy would be desirable from this point of view. But in the unlikely event that a democracy of this extension was actually established, there would be a significant risk of its majority discriminating against one ethnic minority or another. And the fear of this risk makes it improbable that existing nationalist states would give way to a global democracy. (Another reason why a global democracy is unlikely is, of course, that there is no universal endorsement of the ideal of democracy.)

More importantly, even if there were a global democracy, there would still be classes that would be affected by its political decisions, but which would inevitably be without voting power: future generations of human beings and non-human animals. There is a risk that the interests of these classes will be disadvantaged by the political decisions of democratic societies, just as there is a risk that the interests of the classes with less voting power would be disadvantaged were votes weighted. While it is clear what to do to eliminate the latter risk—namely, to give all citizens votes of equal weight—it is less clear what to do to eliminate the risk that the interests of future generations and animals be disadvantaged.[6] Obviously, they could not be given the right to vote in current elections. So, it seems that we have here something of an inescapable shortcoming of democracy, a shortcoming which is amplified by the increasing powers that scientific technology puts in our hands to affect the weal and woe of future people and non-human animals. Therefore, not even the establishment of a global democracy is a guarantee that climatic and environmental problems will be satisfactorily solved. The only possible remedy would seem to be, as we shall argue in the next chapter, that the voters be morally enhanced, by traditional or novel, biomedical methods. In this way, the political decisions of a democracy could be morally improved, though there will be an attendant risk that the discovery of such methods of changing human psychology could be used for opposite purposes, e.g. to create a more servile and morally corruptible populace.

Before we go into this matter, however, we would like to question an assumption that Fukuyama, alongside many other political thinkers back to Plato, seems to take for granted, namely that the form of government which is best will also last indefinitely, or, as he puts it, that it will bring history to an end. Behind this assumption one senses a teleological, Hegelian vision of history as a process destined to end in a perfect state. In order to realize that this is an unwarranted assumption, it is enough to consider that the morally best form of government could quite plausibly endow its citizens with a right to determine the form of government to which they are subject. But then if they do not realize that what is in fact the best government *is* the best government—and they might fail to realize this because a society with the best government does not necessarily have the best of citizens—they might replace it by some other form of government.

In this way, a political order might be too morally good for its own good. It is a well-known fact that individuals might be too morally good for their own good: if they are surrounded by people who are morally unscrupulous, good people risk being exploited and fare badly. Analogously, a state which treats its citizens in a morally exemplary fashion, by giving them extensive rights and liberties and a generous welfare system, etc.—this might be true of liberal democracy, especially in times of prosperity—might fare badly because some citizens take advantage of its goodness, to overthrow it in favour of a political order which is more partial to their own selfish interests, or to make unwise or immoral decisions that are destructive in the longer run.

We suggest that contemporary liberal democracies are in danger of being too liberal to last and that this possibility is particularly serious, given that humans have the capacity to cause Ultimate Harm. In Chapter 4, we suggested that liberal democracies need to become less liberal, by setting aside an (alleged) right to privacy if they are to counteract the threats of terrorists and other crooked individuals with access to weapons of mass destruction. There is, we argued, no moral right to privacy. There is at most a legal right to privacy, which protects interests that could reasonably be regarded as weaker than an interest in the security of life and limb. Such restrictions of liberty is something that the majority could realistically be thought to vote for. In this and preceding chapters, we have contended that liberal democracies will also have to adopt a less liberal attitude to their citizens' resource-consuming way of life if their societies are to survive and prosper in the longer run. It is more doubtful whether the majority will decide to do this unless—as we shall argue in the next chapter—it undergoes a moral enhancement which rectifies the psychological shortcomings, reviewed in Chapter 2, that mar human nature. As scientific technology boosts our powers of action, and our societies have grown to enormous proportions, both with respect to population and economy, these psychological shortcomings become increasingly harmful. Indeed, they risk the very persistence of humanity.

10

Moral Enhancement as a Possible Way Out

If we look back upon the 80,000 years or so that have passed since *Homo sapiens* began to colonize the Earth from Eastern Africa, we discern a process of relentless expansion and exploitation, with very few episodes of restraint. When there has been restraint, the circumstances have been significantly different from those that are now confronting us globally. Societies have been able to adopt sustainable policies, which enabled them and their descendants to overcome ecological threats without colonization or territorial expansion when either (1) these societies were so small that everyone knew everyone else, so that mutual concern and trust were possible, or (2) they featured a wise dictatorial power, which ruled over all their territory and their inhabitants (Diamond, 2005: 277–8, 429).

Obviously, neither of these conditions holds with respect to the re-sources of the Earth. Here it is not only the case that there is a multitude of states competing with each other, there is also a gross inequality in respect of welfare between these nations, with nations in the developing world aspiring to the wealth that Western democracies have enjoyed for so long. It seems unlikely that these deep conflicts could be bridged in the short time at our disposal before we have damaged the global climate and environment irreparably. Therefore, the most likely course of events might well be that we shall walk into some sort of global collapse, the magnitude of which is hard to divine. This is confirmed by the fact that, though climatic and environmental problems have been widely discussed for a couple of decades, and with a special intensity in the last few years, precious little has been done in practice to mitigate appreciably the detrimental anthropogenic impact upon the global climate and environ-ment. This is shown, for example, by the so-called 'Overshoot Day', the day when we have used as much resources as the Earth can regenerate in a year and released as much waste as it can reabsorb in a year. Overshoot day has steadily occurred earlier and earlier in the last couple of decades, and has not recently been pushed back from its alarmingly early occurrence in the year. Since 2008 it is estimated to have occurred in August or September (see *Global Footprint Network*). That is, in a year humans spend close to 30 per cent more than that which the Earth can provide in the same period of time.

There is reason to fear, then, that humankind will follow the fate of previous, now extinct human cultures, like the famous one on Easter Island (Rapa Nui), which have brought about their own downfall by overexploitation of natural resources—a human parallel to the non-human animals, which have been so reproductively successful that they have caused their own populations to collapse. In addition, we must take into consideration a scenario in which shrinking natural resources like oil, arable land, and water may provoke wars with weapons of mass destruction.

Nonetheless, we should not regard a global collapse as inevitable. We are not biologically or genetically determined to go on consuming voraciously, until we are forcibly stopped by the depletion of natural resources. As our history eloquently shows, we are more than any other animal biologically or genetically disposed to learn by experience, and we are now learning that our present course of action spells disaster. We *can* decide to overturn any predictions made about what we will intentionally do because no prediction can take into account the effects that it itself will have.[1]

But, although our behaviour is highly adaptable in the light of experience, some of our behavioural patterns are propelled by quite recalcitrant drives. For instance, it is practically certain that, if the human species does not undergo anything like a dramatic genetic mutation, a majority of humans will not of their own free starve themselves, abstain from sex, and seek utter solitude, whatever their experience seems to teach them. True, some eccentrics might adopt these unusual forms of behaviour, but we can rest assured that they will not spread to the majority of humans. Consequently, we can in practice exclude the possibility of future societies in which these forms of behaviour are the rule.

---

[1] For further discussion of the unpredictability of decisions, see Persson, 2005: ch. 31.

The question now is whether the motivational drives that prod humans to overexploit their environment are too recalcitrant in the majority of them to be hemmed in by an insight into how destructive this conduct is. It is likely that this insight could effect such a behavioural modification in a minority. These people might also be given training in science, which would render them better able to understand the mechanisms behind such phenomena as human induced climate change. This is why it would be possible that there be a meritocracy intent on averting a serious environmental breakdown. But in order for a democracy to avert it, the majority has to be converted. We have seen reasons to believe that this would not be easily achieved, although it is certainly possible because human beings are to a great extent malleable by the norms in the society in which they grow up, and radical social revolutions are conceivable.

Societies have always taken advantage of this fact of human malleability by imprinting upon their subjects moral norms conducive to the survival and prosperity of these societies. The norms inculcated have included not merely norms about refraining from certain types of behaviour, such as killing innocent members of one's own society against their will, or stealing their property, but also norms about making positive contributions to the public good, by helping needy members of one's own community and defending the community against external enemies. Today, when scientific technology has vastly increased our powers of action, and has connected societies all over the world with each other by means of travel and commerce, such intra-societal norms are not nearly enough. Liberal democracies need to inculcate norms that are conducive to the survival and prosperity of a world-community of which their societies are integral parts. They have to take the step from a social liberalism, which acknowledges the need for state interference to neutralize the glaring welfare inequalities within a society, to a *global(ly* responsible) liberalism, which extends welfare concerns globally and into the remote future. This is something that liberal democracies have largely failed to do so far, but it seems necessary that they do so straightaway if they are not to undermine themselves and the living conditions on Earth.[2]

---

[2] There is an especially great risk that the interests of non-human animals, existing in the present or future, be set aside since, apart from the fact that they have no voting power, the moral weight of their interests is more contested. The moral status of non-human animals is an issue that we cannot discuss here, but this should not be taken to imply that we regard it as

This development of liberalism is called for because, as we have repeat-edly stressed, owing to the progress of science, the range of our powers of action has widely outgrown the range of our spontaneous moral attitudes, and created a dangerous mismatch. Environmental problems arise because there is a growing domain, which we could affect by our actions but which is in the periphery of our moral consciousness. To come to grips with these problems we believe that it is necessary to widen the horizons of our moral consciousness. It strikes us as wishful thinking to believe that these problems can be wholly solved by technological innovations like clean fuel and carbon sequestration (contrast Posner, 2004: 160). Even if the carbon emission per unit of GDP produced is cut by as much as 90 per cent until 2050 that would be far from enough to keep the temperature rise at a safe level (Hamilton, 2010: 46). As we have already remarked, human beings have a well-attested propensity to be too optimistic or over-confident about their own abilities and about what they can achieve in the future.

Consider the problem of giving aid to the developing world, discussed in Chapter 4. Here we have had in our possession for a long time the means to eliminate a lot of the starvation and diseases in poor countries, but the will has been lacking to apply these means fully. Likewise, various kinds of cleaner technology exist today—perhaps to such an extent that they could cater for our entire need for energy—but they are not completely implemented. For instance, it is technologically possible to use hydrogen-powered fuel cells as a non-polluting energy source for cars. But there is little demand for such cars because they are much more expensive than internal combustion engine cars powered by petrol, and there are virtually no hydrogen fuelling stations. However, the price on fuel cell cars is not likely to go down, and a sufficient number of fuelling stations are not likely to be built, until the demand for these cars increases. There is, then, something of a catch 22 here.

James Martin speculates, in line with our reasoning in Chapter 8, that because of its 'all-powerful central government', 'low-cost manufacturing', and 'excellent research,' China could quickly start to 'mass-produce and export ecologically benign cars in vast numbers', and thus make an

unimportant. However, since the moral status of non-human animals is contested, we do not want the case for sustainable policies upon it. For a discussion of the threat to biodiversity, see e.g. Wilson, 2002.

enormous profit out of a potentially growing demand for this and other environmental-friendly products (2006: 22–3). But there is an initial obstacle: the protracted transition phase in which the production of such cars will not be profitable because there is not the infrastructure to make them attractive to buyers. So, the Chinese government will probably not have an incentive to change the course of their domestic production. Indeed, this seems to be precisely what is happening as the Chinese government provides petrol at lower cost than the market price to stimulate an automobile revolution of the nation. Another reasonable fear is that instead of developing clean energy, it will fall back upon the enormous coal reserves that China sits upon, though it is comparatively dirty coal. Still, as we have already observed, the future political course of China seems to be harder to predict than that of the US.

Our conclusion is, then, that the solution to climatic and environmental problems is not wholly technological. Nor will there be a political solution in the democratic form of government, unless the will to act morally grows stronger in the public. For these problems have to do with such matters as people being too little concerned about others who are beyond their immediate circle of acquaintances, especially large numbers of such strangers, too much preoccupied with the present and imminent future, and feeling too little responsible for their omissions and collective contributions. Without a willingness to make personal sacrifices for the sake of people in remote countries and in the remote future, there will in all probability not be enough of an effort to develop and put to full use a technology that could arrest or significantly lessen anthropogenic climatic and environmental degradation. To develop this technology requires financial resources that must be extracted in ways that impose costs upon us, like taxes or restrictions on fossil fuels and on certain kinds of food, and to put this technology to use requires our willingness to adopt more costly alternatives to present practices.

Liberal democracies have responded to moral problems in the current global setting by supporting the doctrine of the equality of all humans, e.g. via international organizations like the UN. This egalitarianism is major step forward in comparison to the racism and sexism that were still prevalent in a not very distant past,[3] but this egalitarian ideology has a

---

[3] The Nazi ideology is too familiar to need mentioning; it is more noteworthy that an Oxford philosopher, Hastings Rashdall, a little over a hundred years ago could write

long way to go before it succeeds in stamping out the deep-seated xenophobia of our nature. It is still pretty much of a façade covering an underlying xenophobia which under certain circumstances, e.g. when resources become scarce, breaks out in excessive violence. For instance, this happened in ex-Yugoslavia and Rwanda in the 1990s, and it has more recently happened in Dafur. It is not unreasonable to fear that when crucial natural resources, like oil or water, become scarce in the imminent future, this will cause an outburst of wars with weapons of mass destruction between nations that are 'foreign' or 'out-groups' to each other, racially or religiously.

Moreover, the egalitarian ideology has not pervaded the fundamental domain of economy. Here a Lockean theory of property rights continues to rule the day, even though Locke's own proviso that property acquisition is legitimate only as long as 'there is enough, and as good left in common for others' (1690/1990: II. v. 27) ceased to hold a long time ago. In terms of difference in per capita income between the richest and poorest countries, the world now appears more unequal than it has ever been: 'the difference between the per capita incomes of the richest and the poorest countries was 3 to 1 in 1820, 11 to 1 in 1913, 35 to 1 in 1950, 44 to 1 in 1973, and 72 to 1 in 1992' (Seitz, 2008: 3). At the beginning of the present millennium the wealthiest fifth of the world's population stood for 86 per cent of the world's GDP, while the poorest fifth stood for only 1 per cent of it, and the richest three individuals owned as much as did 600 million people in the poorest countries. Economic inequality in affluent societies, even those with a strong egalitarian ideology, like the Scandinavian countries, increases rather than decreases: for instance, in Sweden the gap between the average salary of a CEO and an average factory worker is now as big as it was in the 1950s after having decreased in the 1960s and 1970s. The tendency in the US is even scarier: the ratio rose from 42:1 in 1960 to a staggering 531:1 in 2000.

To cope with climatic and environmental problems, as well as the problem of global inequality, the ideology of human equality must exercise a stronger motivational influence and overcome the limitations of our altruism and sense of justice. But, to repeat, we must also overcome the

something as blatantly racist as this: 'the lower well being—it may be the very existence—of countless Chinamen or negroes must be sacrificed that a higher life may be possible for a much smaller number of white men' (1907: 238–9).

bias towards the near future, our numbness to the suffering of great numbers, and our weak sense of responsibility for our omissions and collective contributions. It should be asked to what extent this moral enhancement could be accomplished by traditional methods of moral education. These methods include such things as carefully reflecting on the reasons for which actions are morally right or wrong, and making as vivid to oneself as possible how one's actions affect others. This could be made vivid by regularly imagining, actually confronting, or watching films of the suffering victims of wrongdoing. But a ground for suspecting that by such measures moral enhancement could not be accomplished to a sufficient degree in time to avert disastrous misuses of modern technology is that the degree of moral improvement in the 2,500 years that have elapsed since the first great teachers of morality appeared is nowhere near matching the degree of technological progress during the same period.

To bring out this point, it might be helpful to distinguish between improvement in respect of (1) moral doctrines and (2) moral actions and reactions, which requires that improvements in respect of moral doctrine are internalized to the degree that they regulate conduct. We have noted that there have been improvements in respect of moral doctrine to the effect that, for example, racial and sexual differences are now widely regarded as morally irrelevant. It could also be mentioned that punishments in most societies, have become a great deal less barbarous in recent times. Nonetheless, it seems that this improvement has been modest in comparison to the formidable improvement as regards scientific and technological knowledge. By itself this doctrinal difference might not be important, but it assumes greater significance when we add that this scientific and technological knowledge can extend our powers of action by being used to build ever more sophisticated machines and other devices, which can be mastered after a relatively short period of training. In contrast, it is quite hard to internalize moral doctrines to the degree that they determine our behaviour. This is shown not only by how few people live up to more demanding doctrines, for example, those that require the sacrifice of a substantial part of their welfare to save the life of strangers, but more emphatically by the frightening speed with which people, when political conditions allow it, are capable of regressing to barbarous behaviour, which one had hoped humanity had left behind for good. Every new generation has to go through a strenuous moral training anew. Consequently, there is a widening gap between what we are practically able to do, thanks to modern technology, and what we are morally capable of doing, though we might be somewhat more morally capable than our ancestors were. It is this motivational internalization of moral doctrines that we think could be sped up by means which the scientific exploration of the genetic and neurobiological bases of our behaviour might put into our hands. We call moral enhancement by such means *moral bioenhancement*; possible examples of moral bioenhancement would be drug treatment and genetic engineering.[4]

Steven Pinker hypothesizes that 'enhanced powers of reason—specifically, the ability to set aside immediate experience, detach oneself from a parochial vantage point, and frame one's ideas in abstract, universal terms—would lead to better moral commitments' (2011: 656). He believes that the requisite enhanced powers of reason are evidenced by the so-called Flynn Effect, the fact that in the 20th century the IQ has gone up by an average of three points per decade (2011: 650–1). His hypothesis is that this rise could explain 'the documented declines of violence in the second half of the 20th century' (2011: 656): the relatively scarcity of bigger wars and genocide; the marked drop of homicide rates and rates of other violent crimes against women, ethnic minorities, homosexuals, and children; more humane forms of punishment; the recognition of the equal rights of all people irrespective of race and sex; less cruelty to non-human animals; etc.

Now, we do not want to deny that enhanced powers of reason are tremendously important for moral enhancement—perhaps Pinker is right that they are the main force behind the moral improvements that he lists. But we do want to deny that once reason 'is programmed with a basic self-interest and an ability to communicate with others, its own logic will impel it, in the fullness of time, to respect the interests of ever-increasing numbers of others' (2011: 669). We do not see how such an expanding circle of concern is possible without the assistance of the moral dispositions of altruism and a sense of justice. Reason and self-interest could surely tell you to rob and kill an injured stranger in the wilderness rather than help him, or to abstain from returning a favour to someone you will not ever see again rather than to return it at a cost to yourself.

---

[4] For another defence of moral bioenhancement, see Douglas, 2008. For a defence of biomedical enhancement in general, see e.g. Buchanan, 2010.

Pinker suggests that our sympathy or compassion with strangers is too feeble to prod us to make any costlier sacrifices to help strangers even when millions of them are in need of help. True, it is feeble, and there is no way it could be made proportionate to the suffering of millions. But if we had not felt *any* sympathy, we could have paid as little attention to the suffering of millions of people as to the millions of grains of sand stirred up by a gust of wind because neither affects our self-interest. If, however, our sympathy is aroused by the sufferers, we will pause and reflect upon their plight. We will then realize in more detail how horribly great the amount of their suffering is, and our sympathy will receive a boost that could animate us to help them at our own expense. Moreover, if reason informs us that the racial or other differences between one group of individuals for whom we feel sympathy and a sense of justice and another group for which we do not possess these attitudes are insignificant, our sympathy and sense of justice will spread from the former group to the latter. But there can be no such spreading if these attitudes are lacking all together. There-fore, we think that sympathy and a sense of justice are indispensable for being fully moral, and that the explanation of why humanity so far has failed to deal with climate change and environmental destruction—in spite of the enhanced powers of reason—is that they leave self-interest un-touched and call upon our insufficient sympathy and sense of justice as regards future generations and non-human animals.

As we see it, then, the core moral dispositions, which are the foremost objects of moral enhancement, are altruism and a sense of justice as it primarily manifests itself in tit-for-tat. By classifying these as moral dis-positions, we imply that, by themselves, they *always* issue in a morally correct treatment of the individuals to whom they are directed. To be sure, if you are more strongly altruistically disposed towards some indivi-duals than others, this might result in your giving an unfair advantage to the former individuals, but *taken by itself* the behaviour that the strong altruist disposition towards one individual issues in is not morally wrong.[5] In addition, we have also surveyed some cognitive dispositions which are

---

[5] Contrast what for instance Jonathan Haidt, 2003, calls 'moral emotions'. These include for instance 'other-condemning' emotions like anger, contempt, and disgust. Obviously, these can by themselves issue in behaviour against the targeted individuals that is morally wrong. cf. also what Jesse Prinz and Shaun Nichols take to be moral emotions (2010). But even if we do not regard, e.g. anger, as a specifically moral emotion, we do not deny, of course, that a reduction of anger can be a moral improvement.

morally relevant dispositions rather than moral dispositions, like the bias towards the near future and the conception of responsibility as being causally-based. They are morally relevant because they limit the moral dispositions of altruism and justice, but their scope is wider, comprising, for example, self-regarding prudence. What we mean by moral enhancement is first and foremost enhancement of the latter two central moral dispositions, but since the reduction of the bias towards the near future and the conception of responsibility as being causally-based could result in extensions of altruism or the sense of justice, moral enhancement in a wider sense encompasses the reduction of both the temporal bias and the commitment to a causally-based conception of responsibility.

We have suggested that altruism and the sense of justice have biological bases by sketching their evolutionary origin (this does not exclude that they can be influenced also in significant ways by cultural or other social means). But this hypothesis of a biological basis is also supported by studies of animals and identical twins. With respect to animal studies, it is important to make explicit that what we mean by altruism is something else than mere emotional contagion, for example, fear spreading through a herd. It is also something else than the distress and helping behaviour elicited by nothing but the *outward* signs of another's suffering, perhaps for the reason that one finds these signs unpleasant.[6] We have in mind a more sophisticated reaction which involves (1) *empathy*, i.e. a capacity to imagine what it would be like to be another conscious subject and feel its pleasure or pain, etc. as well as (2) *sympathetic concern* about the well-being of this subject for its own sake, e.g. an intrinsic desire to relieve pain, occasioned by the empathic act of imagination. No doubt, it is difficult to tell whether a non-human animal is capable of altruism in this sense, but it seems likely that this is so if an animal exhibits helping behaviour tailored to the individual needs of another animal when these are different from its own needs, such as when a chimpanzee helps a bird to fly (a chimpanzee presumably never experiences any need or desire to fly). Now there is reason to believe that, alongside humans, at least apes and dolphins, and perhaps elephants are capable of altruism in this sophisticated sense. Chimpanzees have often been observed performing acts of low-cost altruism to strangers and acts of

---

[6] Cf. what de Waal calls 'preconcern': 'Preconcern is an attraction toward anyone whose agony affects you. It doesn't require imagining yourself in the other situation' (2010: 96). As we do, de Waal takes genuine sympathetic concern to encapsulate empathy (2010: 88).

high-cost altruism to those who are near and dear (de Waal, 2010: ch. 4). Evidence of dolphin and elephant altruism is less extensive, but existent (de Waal, 2010: 125–39). The occurrence of the tit-for-tat strategy in animals has also been documented. For instance, Frans de Waal has found that, among chimpanzees, 'adults were likely to share food with individuals who had groomed them earlier' (2006: 43; 2010: 173–4). This looks suspiciously like gratitude. In another of his studies, capuchin monkeys (which have the largest brains relative to body size of all monkeys) were paired with a group mate. Their reactions were watched when their partner received a better reward for doing the same bartering task. The different rewards consisted in two kinds of token which could immediately be exchanged for more tasty food, e.g. a grape, and less tasty food, e.g. a piece of cucumber, respectively. De Waal reports:

Individuals who received lower value rewards showed both passive negative reactions (e.g. refusing to exchange the token, ignoring the reward) and active negative reactions (e.g. throwing out the token or the reward). Compared to tests in which both received identical rewards, the capuchins were far less willing to complete the exchange or accept the reward if their partner received a better deal . . . Capuchins refused to participate even more frequently if their partner did not have to work (exchange) to get a better reward but was handed it for 'free' (2006: 47–8).

De Waal concludes: 'Capuchin monkeys thus seem to measure reward in relative terms, comparing their own rewards with those available and their own efforts with those of others' (2006: 48; cf. 2010: 187 ff.). He stresses that the reactions of the capuchin monkeys were rather 'egocentric' (2006: 49) in the sense that they reacted negatively only when they themselves were treated worse, not when their partners got the worse deal. Therefore, it may not be accurate to speak of a sense of fairness without qualification. A proper sense of fairness might require an ability to apply the notion across the board and, so, perhaps presupposes an ability to empathize, as does genuine altruism. According to de Waal, there are indications that chimpanzees exhibit such a sense of fairness (2010: 190–3).

The hypothesis that the sense of justice has a biological basis has been confirmed by studies of human twins playing the roles of proposer and responder in the ultimatum game. Björn Wallace and associates have found that in the case of identical twins (who share the same genes), there is a striking correlation between the average division with respect to both what they propose and what they are ready to accept as responders. There is no such correlation in the case of fraternal twins (2007: 15631–4). This indicates that the human sense of fairness has a genetic basis. According to Simon Baron-Cohen (2003: 114), there is also a striking correlation in respect of altruism in identical twins.

Furthermore, it is plausible to think that in general women have a greater capacity for altruism than men. If a general difference as regards this trait tracks gender, this is good evidence that the trait is biologically based. It has been argued at length by Baron-Cohen (2003) that as rule women have a greater capacity for 'empathy' than men. On our conception of empathy it is, as already remarked, a capacity to imagine vividly what it would be like to be another, to think, perceive, and feel as they do. Thus, as we conceive it, empathy does not involve any motivational component. On this conception, empathy is a merely component of altruism, as we understand it, since we take altruism to include also a motivational component of sympathetic concern about how others feel; a concern that they feel well rather than suffer. This is roughly how Baron-Cohen understands empathy[7] and, so, his claims about empathy can be treated as equivalent to claims about altruism in our terminology.

Baron-Cohen notes that empathy can act as 'brake on aggression' (2003: 35). Thus, we should expect that a lesser male capacity for empathy is likely to go with the greater display of male aggression, which is borne out by the statistics of violent crimes like murder (Baron-Cohen, 2003: 36). Baron-Cohen does not maintain that women are not aggressive at all. His claim is rather that female aggression tends to take the subtler forms of backstabbing, social exclusion, etc. instead of direct physical assault, and these subtler forms of aggression presuppose mind-reading (2003: 35). He also reports that autism, which consists in a deficiency of at least the cognitive or imaginative aspect of empathy, is ten times more common among men (2003: 137). If this is right, it seems that in principle we could make men in general more moral by biomedical methods through making

---

[7] But only roughly, since Baron-Cohen thinks that sympathy is only one example of the affective responses that empathy encompasses (2003: 26–7). This is a disagreement that we need not sort out here.

them more like the men who are more like women in respect of sympathy and aggression, but without the tendency to social forms of aggression.[8]

Some critics of moral bioenhancement have feared that it would be corrosive of freedom and, thereby, of moral responsibility (e.g. Harris, 2011). But this example should make us realize that this fear is misguided: women are not less free and responsible than men because by biological nature they are more altruistic and less aggressive. Suppose, first, that our freedom and responsibility is compatible with it being fully causally determined whether or not we shall do what we take to be good. Then a judicious use of effective techniques of moral bioenhancement to increase a sense of justice and altruism will not reduce our freedom and responsibility; it will simply make it the case that we are more often, perhaps always, causally determined to do what we take to be good. It will do so by amplifying those biological factors that by nature are strong in those of us who are morally better. We would then act as a morally better person now acts. Such a person is not less free and responsible than those of us who more frequently fail to do what we think is morally right.

Suppose, on the other hand, that we are free and responsible only because, by nature, we are not fully causally determined to do what we take to be morally right. Then moral bioenhancement cannot be fully effective because its effectiveness is limited by the indeterministic freedom that we possess. So, irrespective of whether causal determinism or indeterminism reigns in the realm of human action, moral bioenhancement will not curtail human freedom and responsibility. Biomedical manipulation cannot change the basic laws of our behaviour by making us more (or less) causally determined; it simply uses knowledge of those laws to influence our behaviour.

However, some critics of moral bioenhancement seem to think that it would turn us into mindless robots who do not act for reasons. For instance, John Harris writes that moral bioenhancement will 'make the freedom to do immoral things impossible, rather than simply make the doing of them wrong and giving us moral, legal and prudential reasons to refrain' (2011: 105). But, in our view, those who have undergone moral

---

[8] Cf. de Waal: 'I'd be reluctant to radically change the human condition. But if I could change one thing, it would be to expand the range of fellow feeling. The greatest problem today, with so many groups rubbing shoulders on a crowded planet, is excessive loyalty to one's own nation, group, or religion' (2010: 203).

bioenhancement would act for the same reasons as those of us who are most moral today do, and the sense in which it is 'impossible' that they do what they regard as immoral will be the same for the morally enhanced as for the garden-variety virtuous person: it is something that it is psychologically or motivationally out of the question that they choose to do. We imagine that the moral motivation of those of us who are less morally motivated be increased so that it becomes as strong as the moral motivation of those of us who are by nature most morally motivated, not that this moral motivation be increased to the point at which it becomes *irresistible*, like a kleptomaniac's desire to steal. The strength of the desire to do the morally right thing should be proportional to the reasons we have. It is a mistake to believe that people who are by nature morally good and always try to do what they regard as right are necessarily less free and responsible than those of us who more often fail to do so. Just as naturally virtuous people do not compulsively do what they regard as right, so morally enhanced people will not compulsively do what they regard as right.

It is our view that some children should be subjected to moral bioenhancement, just as they are now subjected to traditional moral education. This is because the capacity to influence development under way is likely to be greater than the capacity to alter established motivational dispositions and behaviour. There is no reason to assume that moral bioenhancement to which children are exposed without their consent would restrict their freedom and responsibility more than the traditional moral education to which they are also exposed without their consent. It is of course true that if some children become more morally motivated through bioenhancement, they have not *chosen* to be more moral, but this is also true of the children who become more moral as the result of early moral education and natural endowments. It is quite unlikely that later in life the morally bioenhanced individuals will regret the fact they have undergone this treatment, since otherwise they might have been criminals who would have been punished and condemned by society. Thus, we cannot see that if children are exposed to moral bioenhancement, this will disrupt their freedom and responsibility more than when they are exposed to traditional moral education. As we have already noted, it is not true that they will compulsively do what they think is morally right; nor does moral bioenhancement exclude any options that they would have liked to be open.

It is, however, true that if we come into possession of very effective techniques of bioenhancement, and sharpen the use of traditional moral education, we could determine what motivational states people will be in (if determinism rules in the realm of human behaviour). But this would not imply that these people are not responsible: people can be responsible for how they act and react in situations, even though someone else has determined how they will act and react in those situations. This is true even when the determination takes the form of coercion which restricts the subject's freedom. For instance, if someone forces you to hand over money at gunpoint, you are responsible for giving in to the threat (though this might be perfectly reasonable and not anything for which you are blameworthy). However, when determination amounts to moral enhancement of a person, it does not restrict freedom; it rather extends it, by making the subject more capable of overcoming urges which counteract the doing of what is seen as morally good. This is a point that should be emphasized: when we influence the motivational states of people, this could be liberating rather than constraining. It could be influence of a sort that they have reason to welcome rather than to eschew.

Harris's core claim about freedom, expressed in the idiom of Milton's *Paradise Lost*, seems to be that 'sufficiency to stand is worthless, literally morally bankrupt, without freedom to fall' (2011: 110). In other words, a decision to act in a way that is morally right is morally worthless— meaning, presumably, that you are not morally praiseworthy for it—if you are not free not to make this decision, but instead a decision to do something wrong. This view can be shown to be mistaken by a kind of argument made famous by Harry Frankfurt (1969). Imagine that you decide to do the morally right thing on the basis of considering reasons for and against, as somebody who is morally responsible is supposed to do. Imagine, however, that there is a freaky mechanism in your brain which would have kicked in if you had been in the process of making, not this decision, but a decision to do something which is morally wrong. The mechanism would then irresistibly have made you decide to do the morally right thing. Hence, you are not free to fall, i.e. you cannot avoid deciding to do the morally right thing. Would the presence of this freaky mechanism then mean that you are not praiseworthy for making the right decision? It is hard to see why it would: after all, the mechanism was never called into operation; it remained idle. In fact, you decided to do the morally right thing for precisely the same reasons as someone whose brain does not feature the freaky mechanism could do, and whose praiseworthiness therefore is not in doubt. It seems plausible to think that what determines whether you are morally responsible and praiseworthy is the *actual* occurrences that led up to your decision, not some merely hypothetical occurrences that could have led up to your decision, but in fact did not. Certainly, owing to the presence of the freaky mechanism, you are not free to decide to act immorally; this is not anything you could do. But, as already the example of handing over the money case at gunpoint brings out, freedom of will or action is not indispensable for moral responsibility. So, Harris's 'freedom to fall' is not essential for moral choice and action.

Harris also objects that moral bioenhancement could not be made to target the right sort of motivational states for 'the sorts of traits or dispositions that seem to lead to wickedness or immorality are also the very same ones required not only for virtue but for any sort of moral life at all' (2011: 104). However, a low level of altruism and high level of physical aggression, which lead to immoral behaviour, are not requisite for a moral life. To be sure, a certain amount of aggression might be necessary for moral behaviour: for instance, anger as a response to offences might be necessary to make offenders change their ways. But it should be a degree of anger which is proportionate to the size of the offence, and a sense of justice is required to ensure this, as well as that anger is not directed at people who do not deserve it.[9]

It is somewhat surprising to find Harris among the opponents of moral bioenhancement in view of the fact that he is in favour of cognitive enhancement by means of biomedical methods. A more common attitude is opposition to enhancement of all of our mental or psychological properties by such methods. Discussing cognitive or intellectual bioenhancement in particular, Nick Bostrom and Toby Ord (2006) hypothesize that a main cause of such resistance is a status quo bias, an irrational tendency to prefer a current state of affairs to a change of it simply because it already obtains. We are inclined to think that in many instances the status quo bias is also part of the explanation of the opposition to moral bioenhancement, though this is presumably not so in Harris's case. But, in contrast to Bostrom and Ord, we do not regard the status quo bias as wholly irrational. This is because we link it with the fact that it is easier for us to harm than to benefit because changes to complex systems are more likely to be for the worse rather than for the better. Therefore, it is rational to be cautious

---

[9] For a fuller reply to Harris, see Persson and Savulescu, 2011. See also the reply to Harris by Douglas, forthcoming.

about changing a current state of affairs into something new, and the more radical the change, the more cautious it is rational to be because of the increased risk of unforeseen effects most of which are likely to be for the worse. By contrast, Bostrom and Ord claim that with respect to cognitive enhancements, uncertainty about the consequences 'far from being a sufficient ground for opposing them, is actually a strong consideration in their support' (2006: 669). For the reason already given, we disagree (cf. Agar, 2010: 138–9). On the other hand, it should be admitted that for most of us the status quo bias is too strong, so strong that it often makes us averse to changes for which we have very good reasons. This is especially likely when status quo has obtained for a longer period of time because we have a tendency to form an exceedingly strong emotional bond or attachment to things to which we have grown accustomed.

Since we have been employing the term 'empathy', it should again be underlined that we are here using it in an extended sense, such that empathy includes sympathy or a concern for the well-being of others, not merely imagining what the experiential state of another is like. Psychopaths are known for being skilful manipulators; perhaps this is because they have empathy in the narrower sense of a power to imagine from the inside what it would be like to be another. But they definitely lack sympathy and, so, are not altruists, or empathetic in the more inclusive sense (Baron-Cohen, 2003: 34). Sadists might also have empathy in the less inclusive sense—otherwise they could perhaps not fully enjoy the suffering of another—but they are certainly lacking in sympathy.

Even though it is true that our moral dispositions have a biological basis and, thus, are open in principle to manipulation by biomedical techniques, it does not follow that it is impossible to influence them by moral education. A rough analogy might be this: suppose that we want to improve someone's command of English. To a considerable extent, this might be achieved by exposing the person more to the English language. But at some point improvement by this means begins to level off, and further improvement will occur at best slowly, or not at all, if we do not manipulate the underlying capacity to speak a natural language which presumably is biologically based. Most of us would not acquire the mastery of English of a William Shakespeare or a James Joyce, however much we study the language. Nevertheless, biomedical means are not by themselves sufficient to give someone mastery of English, though they could be necessary for the attainment of certain levels of linguistic competence, or for the attainment of these levels more quickly. This is the sort of role that we think that biomedical means of enhancing altruism and the sense of justice could play if effective such means are discovered.

Education or instruction about what is morally good is not sufficient for moral enhancement because to be morally good involves not just knowing what is good, but also being so strongly motivated to do it that this overpowers selfish, nepotistic, xenophobic, etc., biases and impulses. An instructive comparison could be to people who know perfectly well that they ought not to smoke tobacco or eat sugary and fatty food because it is hazardous to their health, and yet do so out of weakness of will. Techniques of cognitive psychotherapy, such as vividly imagining how awful the harmful consequences of this behaviour could be of help, but might not suffice in all cases. Some individuals might be so strongly genetically disposed to nicotine or sugar addiction that they cannot get out of their addiction without biomedical treatment.

It might be wondered how such treatment could affect our attitudes without affecting our cognitions, but there are everyday experiences that could serve as models. We know that, by overexposure, we could get tired of a sensation or taste that we have hitherto liked and stop liking it, though the sensation or taste remains the same—the phrase 'getting tired of a sensation or taste' implies that the sensation or taste remains the same. Likewise, when people are cured of their irrational fear of spiders, by being exposed first to very small spiders, and successively to larger and larger spiders, until they are able to bear contact with spiders of a size much larger than the ones that used to occasion fear, without feeling fear any longer. There is no reason to think that their perception of those spiders have changed, though their emotional reaction to it has. It is conceivable that a pharmaceutical could cause the chemical changes in our brains underlying these attitudinal changes without our having to undergo any protracted exposure to the relevant stimuli, and suffer the stressful effects that such exposure might bring along. Pharmaceuticals are in fact given to people with agoraphobia or social phobia to reduce their anxiety.

The fact that being moral is not just a matter of possessing some knowledge is, as we have already tried to explain, the reason why the big chasm between our moral and technological capacity has opened up. Theoretical knowledge can be imparted from one generation to the next; thus, it will gradually accumulate over generations, making scientific and technological progress possible. But when people undergo great moral development in the course of their lives, their moral competence will largely die with them. It cannot be transmitted to the next generation as easily as, say, mathematical competence. Nor could moral competence be used to construct devices that will help future generations to be moral in the way mathematics have been used to construct calculating devices. Moral competence is rather like artistic competence. Like artistic progress, moral progress over the generations is considerably slower than technological progress.

Turning now to actual prospects for moral bioenhancement, one of the most promising lines of research has been on the hormone and neurotransmitter oxytocin. Oxytocin is naturally elevated by sex and touching, but it can also be elevated by nasal spray. It facilitates birth and breastfeeding in humans and other mammals, but it also appears to mediate maternal care, pair bonding, and other pro-social attitudes, like trust, sympathy and generosity (Insel et al., 2004).[10] That is why it has been nick-named 'the cuddle hormone'. When oxytocin is administered via nasal spray, it crosses into the brain. Several commonly used drugs are also thought to affect the release or metabolism of oxytocin. For example, the combined oral contraceptive pill, currently used by over 100 million women worldwide, is associated with elevated baseline oxytocin levels and is believed to increase oxytocin secretion. Similarly, glucocorticoids, widely used to treat asthma and other disorders of inflammation, are thought to modulate both the release of oxytocin and the expression of oxytocin receptors in some parts of the brain.

Kosfeld and collaborators investigated the relationship between oxytocin and trust in a simple game of cooperation (Kosfeld et al., 2005). Research subjects were divided into pairs and the first member of the pair (the 'investor') was asked to choose an amount of money to give to the second member (the 'trustee'), knowing that the second member will receive three times the amount of money given. The second member then chooses an amount of money to return to the first member. The initial payment can thus be viewed as a signal of trust, while the return payment

---

[10] Here we cannot resist quoting the sagacious remarked by Tsutomu Yamaguchi who survived the atomic blasts both at Hiroshima and Nagasaki: 'The only people who should be allowed to govern countries with nuclear weapons are mothers, those who are still breast-feeding their babies' (D. Garner: 'After the atom bomb's shock, the real horrors began unfolding', *New York Times*, 20 January 2010.)

can be interpreted as an indication of trustworthiness and gratitude. A greater level of trust signalled by the investor increases the total amount of money to be allocated between the two players, but the investor benefits from this only to the extent that the trustee is trustworthy and grateful. Prior to playing the game, participants were randomized to receive a nasal spray containing either oxytocin or placebo. Investors administered oxytocin exhibited significantly more trusting behaviour— that is, they entrusted the trustee with a significantly greater amount of money.

In a similar game to that to used by Kosfeld, Zak and associates found that the perception of a sign of trust by the trustee is accompanied by a spike in oxytocin levels and that the degree of trustworthiness exhibited by the trustee is positively and significantly correlated with the oxytocin level (Zak et al., 2004). Thus, in a population with universally elevated oxytocin levels increased trusting behaviour seems to be matched by increased trustworthiness.

However, oxytocin's effects on trust and other pro-social behaviour towards others appears to be sensitive to the group membership of these others. A research team led by de Dreu presented participants who had been randomized to receive either oxytocin or placebo via nasal spray with moral dilemma scenarios in which one individual would have to be sacrificed in order to save a greater number (de Dreu et al., 2011). Participants administered oxytocin were significantly more likely to sacrifice a different-race individual in order to save a group of race-unspecified others than they were to sacrifice a same-race individual in the same circumstances. In participants who had been administered a placebo, the likelihood of sacrificing an individual did not significantly depend on the racial group of the individual. The suggestion is that the pro-social effects of oxytocin may be limited to in-group members and exclude out-groups.

Further experiments by de Dreu's group indicated that oxytocin can also *reduce* pro-social behaviour towards out-group individuals where this helps one's in-group. Administration of oxytocin prior to participating in a group-based financial game induced 'tend and defend' reactions: it increased trust and cooperation within groups, but also increased non-cooperation with—though not offensive aggression against—members of other groups when this helped to protect one's in-group (de Dreu et al., 2010).

This work supports the hypothesis that the pro-social effects of oxytocin are more accurately characterized as 'pro-in-group' effects, since the hormone can in fact induce antisocial behaviour when this conduces to the interests of one's in-group. Thus, it might be that a higher level of oxytocin amplifies the intensity of trust and reciprocity within an already favoured group rather than extends their range to out-groups. Since in-group favouritism seems to drive class and racial discrimination, which in extreme cases manifests itself in genocide and terrorism, administration of oxytocin would not by itself be an effective cure against these evils. It would have to go hand in hand with reasoning which undercuts race, sex etc. as grounds for moral differentiation. But that oxytocin by itself does not suffice for requisite moral enhancement does not show that it cannot be an indispensable aid.

To proceed to another class of current pharmaceuticals which have moral effects, selective serotonin reuptake inhibitors (SSRIs) are commonly prescribed for depression, anxiety, and obsessive compulsive disorder. They help govern activities such as eating and sleeping, and sexual activity. Millions of people world-wide use these drugs. SSRIs work by slowing the reabsorption of serotonin, a neurotransmitter crucially involved in mood, thereby making more of it available to stimulate receptors. Now SSRIs seem to make subjects more fair-minded and willing to cooperate. Tse and Bond (2002) had subjects play the dictator game—a game in which a dictator decides how a certain sum of money is to be divided between him or her and another participant—and found that subjects administered the SSRI citalopram divided the sum more fairly than controls. Conversely, depletion of a precursor of serotonin, tryptophan, which would lead to reduced levels of serotonin, brought along lower rates of cooperation in the prisoners' dilemma game (Wood et al., 2006). The effect was only evident for subjects with depleted tryptophan in the first round of testing, suggesting that serotonin contributes to establishing a cooperative pattern of response, not maintaining it.

In the ultimatum game previously described, normal human subjects typically reject offers they regard as grossly unfair, despite the fact that rejection decreases their pay-off (in a one-shot game). Crockett and colleagues (2008) found that depletion of tryptophan led to increased rates of rejection of unfair offers relative to controls. This suggests that SSRIs may make subjects easier to exploit by modulating their assessment of what counts as (unacceptably) unfair. However, it is not clear how an increased rate of rejection of unfair offers is to be interpreted: does it really signify a heightened sense of (un)fairness, or just greater aggressiveness and irascibility, which increase the probability that people will actually protest against what they see as unfairness? In any case it is clear that modifications of the brain by drugs like SSRIs have moral consequences.

The example of oxytocin and serotonin both show that manipulations of biology can have moral effects. There are then prospects of moral bioenhancement, even if so far no biomedical means of moral enhancement with sufficiently precise effects have been discovered, and perhaps they will never be. However, it is not surprising that no straightforward moral enhancers have hitherto been discovered because research into moral enhancement is a tiny field that is only a few years old.

Even if such means were discovered, the daunting task of applying them to a sufficient number of people—probably in the range of hundreds of millions—would remain. In any event, we are not envisaging that moral bioenhancement will ever reach a point at which traditional methods of moral education—or other social strategies like institutional redesign using incentives—will be redundant. As already explained, we think that these methods will need to be used as well and, indeed, that they should be employed more extensively than they are today. We are here highlighting biomedical means of moral enhancement because many people reject them for bad reasons, such as that they inevitably undercut freedom and responsibility. If effective, biomedical means could presumably be employed in a fashion that they undermine freedom and responsibility, but so could more traditional means if the application of them is so intense that it amounts to brainwashing.

In our view it is a serious mistake to reject moral bioenhancement out of hand because the need for human moral enhancement is so acute that we should not write off any potentially effective means without thorough examination. Significant moral enhancement of the human species appears to be necessary in order to ensure the survival of human civilization in the longer run. But many of us are loath to acknowledge that we are in need of moral improvement; it hurts our pride to acknowledge our moral deficiencies and, as consequence, to shoulder a possibly burdensome duty to rid ourselves of these deficiencies. It is more convenient to believe that the solution to the overwhelming problems of our time that we have outlined in this book is external to us and could be found either in technological inventions or political institutions like democracy. But these external instruments cannot handle the threats to the future of our civilization, unless they controlled by morally responsible people.

Although a great deal of moral improvement is hard going, it should be noted that some of it could be achieved quite easily because human beings are so prone to conformism. It is likely that merely by letting children grow up in a more altruistic environment they will become more altruistic. Indeed, it has been found that people are so readily influenced that just making them perform the task of unscrambling sentences about helpfulness increased their tendency to perform low-cost altruistic acts, such as picking up dropped objects (Macrae and Johnston, 1998). Certainly, such effects are only temporary. By contrast, having children grow up in a more altruist society, which discourages preferential treatment of friends and relatives to a greater extent than is present in liberal societies, is likely to have a lasting effect upon their altruistic proclivities. Thus, if a spirit of altruism began to spread in a community, this process could accelerate leading to societies with progressively more altruistic norms.

However, liberal democracies might be opposed to the implementation of more thorough-going programmes of moral education because it is at odds with the ideal that the state should strive for ideological and evaluative neutrality. Liberalism is based upon the doctrine of negative rights which, as we have suggested, we are designed by evolution to endorse. The main function of the state is taken to be to guard these rights. For instance, this doctrine of rights appears to be behind J. S. Mill's famous principle of liberty, according to which the only legitimate reason for state inference is harm to others, benefits to the self being insufficient to justify this measure. If injuring *any* interest of another were to count as harm, this principle could legitimize state interference against virtually all actions. So, Mill suggests a restriction to 'certain interests which, either by express legal provision or by tacit understanding, ought to be considered as rights' (1859/1978: 73). These interests will presumably turn out to be the ones that common sense takes to be protected by negative rights. According to the argument in Chapter 4, this would disqualify the contravention of all interests, which results in merely 'belief-mediated' distress.

But traditional liberalism has been too permissive as regards letting citizens of affluent societies adopt ways of living that waste the resources of the planet. We have suggested that so far all viable societies have inculcated something like the common-sense morality that we outlined in Chapter 2. This morality might have been conducive to the good of these societies through preceding human history. However, it is too restricted in the current globalized setting of societies with advanced technology. This setting necessitates the inculcation of norms that are conducive to the good of the world community of which these societies are an integral part. Since such a revised morality goes beyond the morality to which we are naturally inclined, moral training will have to be more thoroughgoing and pursued intensively in school from the start.

It might be objected that we are proposing to imprint upon the public a morality that is philosophically controversial. Certainly, our scepticism of moral rights and causally-based responsibility is philosophically controversial. But it is not controversial to think that the limitation of our altruism to those who are near and dear, the bias towards the near future, and the numbness to larger numbers of sufferers are unjustifiable. The morality that we are proposing is to this extent a rather modest extension of common-sense morality, an extension which puts greater emphasis upon duties that common-sense morality already recognizes, in particular the duty to benefit those in need. The moral enhancement that we are recommending is largely a matter of motivating ourselves to do what we already believe to be right, of overcoming our moral weakness of will. However, if it is not accepted that that which we single out as morality is all of what remains of what is commonly called morality when it has been subjected to rational criticism, we could resort to stipulation and say that what we single out are those elements of morality—i.e. those doctrines which are about the well-being of other beings—that are of particular importance to the solution of the global problems that we have presented.

It should however be frankly admitted that moral bioenhancement worthy of the name is practically impossible at present and might remain so for so long that we will not master it, nor succeed in applying it on a sufficient scale, in time to help us to deal with the catastrophic problems that we have outlined. But our point is just that the predicament of humankind is so serious that all possible ways out of it should be explored. Therefore, it is important that moral bioenhancement is not written off without good reason. Because of the gravity of the current human predicament, effective moral bioenhancement, were it technically feasible, would in our view be the most important kind of biomedical enhancement.

However, it must not be forgotten that the techniques of moral bioenhancement raise the same moral problems that all powerful technological innovations create: how to ensure a wise and proper application of them.

All technology is liable to the dual use problem: they can be put to both beneficial and harmful uses. In the case of techniques of moral bioenhancement, this takes the form of a bootstrapping problem: it is human beings, who themselves need to be morally enhanced, who have to (a) be enough interested in being morally enhanced to set aside sufficient resources for research into biomedical means of moral enhancement, and (b) if effective biomedical means are discovered, to make a morally wise use of them. We see no reason to think that this research need be so costly that (a) would be a problem. In our opinion it is (b) which presents the greatest problem: is to hope for a wise use of biomedical means of moral enhancement not to hope for too much when humans have made such unwise use of so much scientific technology? We have already warned against the tendency to be overconfident about what we can achieve in the future by yet to be discovered means; so, we must be careful not to pin our hopes to high. But, on the other hand, there is the opposite risk that too much pessimism about the possibility of moral bioenhancement could lead to it being prematurely dropped from the agenda.

Morally enhancing the majority of people in modern democracies is certainly a huge task. But we are not assuming that such an enhancement will have to be accomplished by biomedical means alone. Traditional moral education also has a part to play, perhaps the largest part. These means of moral enhancement could interact with the impact of social and political reforms that have greater chances of gaining democratic voters' support once there has been some measure of moral enhancement. Thus, we are imagining an interplay between biomedical and social/political techniques rather than the former being alone in the driver's seat. But, since the discovery of effective techniques of moral bioenhancement still lies far ahead, it is difficult to envisage what form a large-scale application of them should assume. And, indeed, it might turn out that such an application is never needed because it has been pre-empted by other means; traditional means of moral enhancement or institutional means (or because human civilization has been ruined). With respect to some of the obstacles to moral behaviour that we have discussed, like the conception of responsibility as being causally-based, the bias towards the near and the availability bias, we are not familiar with any other kind of remedy than a traditional, cognitive one.

Irrespective of whether the means of moral enhancement be traditional or biomedical, they will scarcely be enough, given the gravity of the problems that we have described: it is likely that we will also have to accept a rather extensive surveillance by the state, since there will inevitably be a few individuals among us who are bent upon using the powerful means of scientific technology to wreak havoc. Moral enhancement could not realistically prevent there being a small number of morally warped individuals deploying powerful technology for nefarious purposes. Therefore, we think that the application of means of surveillance of citizens which go beyond those used in the fight against traditional crimes are necessary. These means involve setting aside what people in liberal democracies have come to regard as rights, in particular the right to privacy. Likewise, the freedom of media needs to be restricted with respect to the publication of scientific studies that could supply terrorists with horrific weapons, as illustrated by the mousepox case discussed in Chapter 4. But moral education also has a role to play in this context, for instance, to combat xenophobia which might flare up against ethnic groups some of whose members have committed acts of terrorism. However, some shortcomings of a cognitive sort need to be corrected, in particular the availability bias. Otherwise, people will be inclined to exaggerate the risk of future terrorist acts of a kind that they have already experienced and be blind to the possibility of other kinds.

It seems nowadays to be a common assumption that science could provide a cure for more or less all of the serious problems that humanity faces. This belief is encouraged by the fact that, thanks to science, in affluent societies more people lead longer and better lives than ever before in human history. But there is a non-negligible risk that, as science probes deeper and deeper into nature, science will unleash some highly destructive, uncontrollable processes. Rees (2003) mentions the risks of powerful particle accelerators, like the one in the CERN laboratory in Geneva, of runaway gene-modified organisms and self-replicating, omnivorous nanomachines. Nanotechnology illustrates the dilemma well. On the one hand, there is the hope, for instance, that it could play a central role in counteracting global warming by creating nanomachines which devour carbon dioxide molecules in the atmosphere. On the other hand, this could let loose uncontrollable, self-replicating, and omnivorous nanomachines.

So, scientific progress undoubtedly generates catastrophic risks. But if it were brought to a halt—this certainly stretches the imagination—this might mean that we divest ourselves of the possibility of dealing with other catastrophic risks, which already exist and which we could otherwise have disarmed. An example of such a kind of risk is the risk of asteroid strikes. Some 65 millions ago an asteroid hit Earth, and it is commonly believed to have rubbed out the dinosaurs and many other life forms. This asteroid is estimated to have been 10 km in diameter, and asteroids of this size or more are expected to hit the Earth only once in 50 to 100 million years. But collisions with smaller asteroids, with a diameter of 1.5 to 2 km, might kill a billion people or more, and they are expected to occur roughly twice in a million years (Posner, 2004: 25–6).

Approximately 75,000 years ago a volcano erupted in Toba, Indonesia. As a result of the tremendous quantities of sunlight-blocking ash it spewed out into the atmosphere, the global temperature dropped by 5–15°C. It is surmised that the human population shrunk to around 4,000 reproductive individuals (Rampino, 2008: 211–12). According to some estimates, such super-eruptions occur once in 50,000 years. There is therefore reason to try to predict them and to take precautions against them.

However, it seems clear that the prospect of reducing the risk of such mega-threats could not outweigh the mega-threats that scientific progress has generated. In terms of mega-threats the balance comes out against contemporary science and technology. Rees judges that 'the odds are no better than fifty-fifty that our present civilisation on the Earth will survive to the end of the present century' (2003: 8). Such an estimate would have been wildly implausible with respect to any other hundred year period before 1950s, the time at which humans acquired the nuclear capacity to blow up the Earth.[11] At that time, the power to cause Ultimate Harm lay in the hands of only a few; today it is in the hands of many more, and the number is likely to grow. Consequently, it seems indisputable that contemporary scientific technology has increased the risk of world-wide catastrophe, even if it is the case that Rees's estimate of the risk is somewhat exaggerated. Worse still, if the progress of scientific technology continues, and there is no moral enhancement of human beings, the probability that civilization will survive not just the present century, but also the following centuries will be progressively lower. This is a horrifying trend that must be broken.

---

[11] It should also be remarked, that around 1950, the human population on Earth was still only 2.5 billion, so the catastrophic degradation of the environment had not yet gained momentum.

We are inclined to believe that at the time, half a century ago or so, when scientific technology provided us with means of causing Ultimate Harm, technological development reached a stage at which it became worse *all things considered* for us to have the current means of scientific technology, given that we are not capable of handling them in a morally responsible way. If life on this planet were to end soon in a catastrophe caused by modern technology, when it would otherwise have continued for millennia, the final judgement will have to be that the present technological development has been for the worse all things considered. It is possible that there was a turning point in the development of scientific technology, that at some point—of course not a very precise point—it turned from being for the better all things considered to being for the worse all things considered. We believe that such a turning point could have been when it provided us with means of causing Ultimate Harm. Thus, we do not wish to commit ourselves to the extreme claim that technological development *from its inception,* in Stone Age, say, has been for the worse all things considered.

Nonetheless, this extreme claim might not be so grotesquely implausible as it might seem at first sight. For instance, Craig Dilworth writes:

it may be suggested that the Upper Palaeolithic (40,000–25,000 BP) constitutes the high point in the human way of life to date . . . it can fairly be said that we never had it so good before, and we've never had it so good since. Though average longevity was short by modern Western standards, those who survived infanticide and death related to protowar lived to an advanced age, 60 to 70 being quite possible. (2010: 204)

Dilworth notes that people at this time, at the beginning of human technology, were well nourished, since big game was plentiful, and suffered very few diseases. Most of our infectious diseases come from domesticated animals; according to Dilworth, 'humans now share 65 diseases with dogs, 50 with cattle, 46 with sheep and goats, and 42 with pigs' (2010: 244). At the time in question the domestication of animals had not yet started. Nor were these hunter-gatherers afflicted by diseases related to tobacco smoking, obesity, and pollution, which claim many lives today.

Consequently, if we compare the *average* sum of welfare of human life, it may not be much higher today, for although many people in contemporary affluent societies have a higher quality of life than Cro-Magnons—because they enjoy the blessings of modern technology and culture—at least as many in developing countries lead lives that are of lower quality because they starve and are plagued by a plethora of diseases. What is striking, then, is that the extraordinary technological advance has done comparatively little to raise this average. There are at least two reasons for this. First, the profusion of material wealth that this advance has generated has created large problems of distribution, which we have been incapable of handling. Secondly, a considerable portion of the products that this advance has yielded serves the function of remedying defects that this advance itself has given rise to. This is consonant with our claim about the urgent need for moral enhancement, in order to ensure a morally wiser use of this advanced technology.

Of course, if we consider the *total sum* of human welfare instead of its average level, it is vastly greater today than in the days of Cro-Magnon, since the human population is now more than a thousand times bigger. But the huge amount of current human welfare might be bought at the price of less human welfare in the future, since we are now depleting the resources of the planet.[12] And in any case, the goodness of an outcome is determined not just by the total sum of its welfare—as the so-called repugnant conclusion brings out (see Parfit, 1984: ch. 17)—we need also to consider its quality, as well as the justice of its distribution. The general point is, however, just that it should not be assumed that average improvements as regards human life quality or welfare automatically march in step with technological progress. It should not be taken for granted that just because the technology of a society is primitive the average quality of life in it is poor.

However, in one respect there has been clear change to the better in the course of human history: the percentage of people who suffer violent deaths—and from other acts of violence such as torture and rape— has gone down considerably since prehistoric times, with the switch from non-state to state societies and the subsequent growth of commerce and trade.[13] Hence, Dilworth's caveat 'those who survived infanticide and

---

[12] In this respect there is a parallel between the present time and the period Dilworth describes because the welfare of the Cro-Magnons came at the expense of the mayhem they inflicted upon the mega-fauna of newly colonized territory. Although, as Pinker notes (2011: 454–74), there has recently been progress in the recognition of animal rights or welfare; the expansion of the meat industry and the loss of biodiversity mean that humans kill animals at a faster rate than ever.

[13] As forcefully argued by Pinker, 2011: esp. chs. 2 and 3.

death related to protowar'.[14] The decline of the proportional number of acts of violence is a necessary accompaniment of the enlargement of human societies from around 100 members to millions and even billions of members. Such huge societies could not exist without an authority in possession of a monopoly on violence, which effectively curbs the aggressiveness of their citizens. Furthermore, the thick web of trade and commerce inside these societies and between human societies all over the world has produced a level of welfare that people are reluctant to put at risk by starting violent conflicts. International commerce, alongside the devastating power of modern weapons—both fruits of advanced scientific technology—act as powerful war deterrents, by boosting the costs of waging war.

But we cannot rest assured that this pacification process will continue. A threatening depletion of natural resources could raise the prospect of gain by predatory wars sufficiently to make it worthwhile in the eyes of national leaders. Moreover, religion continues to pose a risk because by promising rewards in an afterlife it could justify wars which in terms of this world are ruinous for all parties. Perhaps it is less likely that nation states will wage wars on purely religious grounds, but then we should keep in mind that, if not already in the present, at least in the near future, small groups or even single individuals may be in possession of devastating weapons of mass destruction, and they might well be fanatical enough to put them to full use, though from a worldly perspective they, along with everyone else, will lose out.

Thus, against the decreasing incidence of violent outbreaks, on individual and national levels, we must set the enormously greater destructive potential of an individual instance. The number of humans who die at the hands of their fellows is a function not only of (a) how many times their fellows engage in acts of killing, but also of (b) the effectiveness of the weapons or means of killing that they then use. We agree that, proportionally, the number of occasions when humans engage in acts of killing has gone down, but the weapons that they have at their disposal are more effective than ever and are likely to be even more effective in the future. So, we cannot be confident that, because people in general have become less prone to indulge in killings and other forms of violence,

---

[14] We bracket the reduction of infanticide, since it bears as little on the issue of pacification as does the high percentage of pregnancies that nowadays end in abortion.

the percentage of victims of human killing will remain comparatively low as e.g. the victims of rape—where the (b)-factor is negligible—presumably will.

However, irrespective of what the upshot of this risk assessment of the development of science and technology is, it is beyond question that this development has made our moral responsibility, including our responsibility for handling the risks that we encounter, larger than it has ever been. An age of powerful scientific technology is inescapably also an age of wide-ranging moral responsibility; with power of action comes responsibility. Once we gain the power to alter nature's course, we become responsible for allowing nature to take the course it takes. Thus, there is a moral gulf between accepting what nature delivered when there was nothing that we could do about it and accepting what nature delivers when we can affect the course of nature: in the latter case we are responsible for letting it happen and must morally justify our stand.

The fact that it is easier to harm than to benefit accentuates how important it is that our behaviour is under moral control, as well factually informed. As our powers of action are enlarged by scientific technology, our capacity to harm grows more than our capacity to do good. In the pre-scientific past many of the risks with which the world presented us were ones that we could not do anything about. Now we can to a considerable extent do something about the risks we face, by applying knowledge that science yields. Thus, we are able to do a lot of good, but we might be responsible for even more harm, by active designs or omissions, since it is easier to harm than to benefit. In a democracy the responsibility to decide ultimately falls upon the shoulders of the voters, and they should be morally fostered and scientifically informed to carry it well. Wise decisions require not only good scientific knowledge but also internalization of a robust and well-grounded set of moral values.

There is an explosion of possibilities of scientific research, and it is getting increasingly important to be keenly selective and give priority to research which is most beneficial to human beings and other organisms on Earth. As things stand at present, research is rather directed by the interest of the most privileged to have further economic growth and greater affluence. This is leading to a depletion of natural resources, a reckless release of waste products, and a widening of the gap between the best and the worst off people. What is needed is what might be called a 'science-sophy', moral wisdom as regards the pursuit of scientific research and its practical applications. Alongside moral judiciousness, this wisdom involves a good measure of scientific knowledge: in a modern democratic society in which political decisions involve a lot of science, it is desirable that the general public and politicians possess a reasonable knowledge of science. According to such a science-sophy, the clearest example of scientific research that we should not engage is probably military and armament research, which consumes gigantic resources, even in the poorest nations, such as North Korea.

A different sort of example of arguably misguided research might be research into the possibility of extending human longevity beyond the 120 years or so now thought feasible. Such research tends to increase the acute population problems that already exist, and to enlarge the huge gap in life-expectancy that already obtains between people in the developed and the developing nations. A science-sophy would recommend moral bioenhancement rather than any other kind of enhancement. Generally speaking, scientific research should be informed by a global, number-sensitive altruism and sense of justice which is not temporally biased, or reigned in by a conception of responsibility as causally-based. By contrast, much contemporary research remains governed by the selfish interests of the rich, which aggravates global inequality and harms the interests of future generations.

It is a naïve illusion to think that we could eventually rid ourselves of the necessity of having to make morally hard decisions with respect to science because it will in the future enable us to do everything we want. Even if, as is most unlikely, science were to develop, for example, to a point at which it would allow us to take care of all present climatic and environmental problems (at least in so far as they affect human welfare), without our having to restrain our consumerist lifestyle, or radically reduce our number, there would still be the moral problem of how to handle the risks of intentional misuses of this science which will have to be exceedingly powerful. In general, scientific progress could not relieve us of moral responsibility; instead, it inevitably extends its range. Any powerful technology is liable to the dual use problem, and since it is easier to harm than to benefit, it is most likely that it can be misused to create greater harm than it can do good.

Consider, for instance, a geoengineering scheme aimed at keeping the temperature of the Earth down by increasing the extent to which its atmosphere reflects incoming solar radiation. This could be done by injecting sulphur dioxide gas into the stratosphere to create sulphate aerosols, particles that reflect solar radiation. Carbon dioxide could then accumulate in the atmosphere without any temperature rise. While this scheme would counteract a temperature increase, it would have an opposite effect on the acidification of the oceans which is due to their absorption of carbon dioxide from the atmosphere. This increasing acidification would lead to a dissolution of coral reefs. According to some conjectures, the injection of sulphur dioxide into the stratosphere would also disrupt the Asian and African summer monsoons, which could jeopardize the food production for billions (Hamilton, 2010: 177). However, the most worrying aspect of such an ambitious piece of climate engineering is that, as a large-scale measure that has never been tried out, it is bound to have unknown side effects, and these are more likely to be harmful than beneficial, since it is easier to damage a functioning system than to improve upon it. But once we have started to inject sulphur dioxide in the stratosphere to keep the temperature down, we are trapped: if we observe untoward effects, we cannot discontinue these injections without causing a devastating temperature jump (Hamilton, 2010: 182). Moreover, we have not got around the difficulty of securing international agreements. Different nations are likely to want to set the global 'thermostat' differently, e.g. China is likely to want to set it lower than Russia. Consequently, serious international conflicts over the 'ideal' global temperature might result (Hamilton, 2010: 182–3).

All the same, since so little is currently done to reduce the emission of greenhouse gases, we must calculate with a situation in which humanity will resort to large-scale geoengineering to avoid climate disaster. It is desirable that we are well prepared for such an emergency by having as carefully as possible investigated the pros and cons of different techniques of geoengineering. Some have objected that if we open up the prospect of geoengineering, this encourages the current slackness about reducing the emission of greenhouse gases. In our opinion, however, this slackness is already so great that the risk of increasing it somewhat cannot do much damage.

However, we believe that moral enhancement, by traditional means as well as novel means that biomedical research is likely to unearth, has priority. This is not just with respect to bringing about a willingness to stop deleterious climate change. We have seen that we need a very advanced technology—in all probability a more advanced technology than we already possess—in order to provide the enormous, and increasing, human population with a decent standard of life without exhausting the resources of the planet. But it is vain to hope for a technological fix that by itself solves this equation. Without moral restraint it is likely that, as has happened in the past, a more efficient technology will be spent on a further expansion of human activities (a tendency elaborated at great length by Dilworth, 2010). Moreover, since it is easier to harm than to benefit, more efficient technology will bring in its wake a greater risk of Ultimate Harm. Thus, we face a dilemma with respect technological progress which only moral enhancement can take us out of: we need it to improve the lot of humanity, but it brings along a risk of Ultimate Harm. In our view, moral enhancement is necessary if human civilization is to have a reasonable chance of surviving not merely the present century but also following centuries.

We shall not attempt to predict whether, by one means or another, liberal democracies will ever come to possess sufficient moral wisdom in the employment of scientific technology, or whether they will rather founder on the problems generated by this technology. Our main point is merely that liberal democracies are in need of moral enhancement in order to deal safely with the overwhelming power of modern technology. It is crucial that we be aware of the moral limitations of our nature, and do whatever we can to correct these limitations, by traditional or new scientific means. We are not trying to predict to what extent we shall in fact succeed in rectifying these limitations in time, or what the future of humanity will in fact be. This is because we are of the opinion that the future of humanity cannot be reliably predicted; at best, we can predict roughly what is likely to happen *if* various policies are adopted. As already remarked, this is because we have the capacity to overturn categorical predictions that we make by making decisions on the basis of them. But even conditional predictions of larger scale outcomes are highly unreliable because these outcomes depend upon innumerable small factors, each of which could have big effects on the future. Imagine, for instance, how different the world might have been if Al Gore instead of George W. Bush had been declared the winner of the tight US Presidential election of 2000.

In conclusion, more efficient technology seems necessary to provide the huge human population on Earth with an acceptable living standard without wearing out the planet. Nevertheless, since it is easier to harm than to benefit, there is likely to be a turning point at which the growth of human powers of action by means of scientific technology becomes for the worse, all things considered, because the moral shortcomings of humankind make the risks of catastrophic misuses of these powers too great. These risks are real because human psychology and morality are adapted to life in small, close-knit communities with simple technology, not the societies with millions of citizens and an advanced scientific technology that we find today. Simply because the human population is larger than ever, immoral actions occur more frequently today than ever, and with potentially more disastrous consequences because of the enormous number of agents and the means of modern technology.

We believe that a turning point was passed at least some fifty years ago when humans acquired the means of causing Ultimate Harm by nuclear weapons. However, it is possible for humankind to improve morally to the extent that the possession of the overwhelming powers of action supplied by scientific technology could be used to create an unprecedented amount of human—and animal—welfare. This is a definite possibility, not least because biomedical techniques that could be provided by the advance of science, along with the techniques of traditional moral education, could be employed to promote a moral enhancement of humankind. But we are not in the business of trying to predict whether or not a happy ending is likelier than a catastrophic outcome, nor what, if anything, will in the end be the most effective means to such a happy ending.

Bibliography

Ackerman, Gary and Potter, William C. (2008), 'Catastrophic Nuclear Terrorism: A Preventable Peril', in N. Bostrom and M. Ćirković (eds.), *Global Catastrophic Risks* (Oxford: Oxford University Press).

Agar, Nicholas (2010), *Humanity's End* (Cambridge, MA: MIT Press).

Alloy, L. B. and Abramson, L. Y. (1979), 'Judgment of Contingency in Depressed and Nondepressed Students: Sadder but Wiser?', *Journal of Experimental Psychology: General* 108: 441–85.

Baron-Cohen, Simon (2003), *The Essential Difference: Male and Female Brains and the Truth about Autism* (New York: Basic Books).

Benatar, David (2006), *Better Never to Have Been* (Oxford: Clarendon Press).

Bostrom, N. and Ćirković, M. (eds.) (2008), *Global Catastrophic Risks* (Oxford: Oxford Uuniversity Press).

——and Ord, T. (2006), 'The Reversal Test: Eliminating the Status Quo Bias in Applied Ethics', *Ethics* 116: 656–79.

Buchanan, Allen (2010), *Beyond Humanity?* (Oxford: Oxford University Press).

Butler, Joseph (1726/1969), *Fifteen Sermons*, reprinted in D. D. Raphael (ed.), *British Moralists*, vol. I. (Oxford: Oxford Univeristy Press).

Crockett, M. J., Clark, L., Tabibnia, G., Lieberman, M. D., and Robbins, T. W. (2008), 'Serotonin Modulates Behavioral Reactions to Unfairness', *Science* 320: 1739.

de Dreu, Carsten et al. (2010), 'Neuropeptide Oxytocin Regulates Parochial Altruism in Intergroup Conflicts among Humans', *Science* 328: 1408–11.

——(2011), 'Oxytocin Promotes Human Ethnocentrism', *PNAS,* 108, 1262–6.

de Waal, Frans (2006), *Primates and Philosophers*, ed. S. Macedo and J. Ober (Princeton, NJ: Princeton University Press).

——(2010), *The Age of Empathy* (London: Souvenir Press).

Diamond, Jared (2005), *Collapse* (London: Penguin Books).

Dilworth, Craig (2010), *Too Smart for Our Own Good* (Cambridge: Cambridge University Press).

Dobson, K. and Franche R. L. (1989), 'A Conceptual and Empirical Review of the Depressive Realism Hypothesis', *Canadian Journal of Behavioural Science* 21: 419–33.

Douglas, Thomas (2008), 'Moral Enhancement', *Journal of Applied Philosophy* 25: 228–45.

——(forthcoming), 'Moral Enhancement via Direct Emotion Modulation: A Reply to John Harris', *Bioethics*.

Douglas, Thomas and Savulescu, J. (2010), 'Synthetic Biology and the Ethics of Knowledge', *Journal of Medical Ethics* 36: 687–93.

Dunning, D., Heath, C., and Suls, J. (2004), 'Flawed Self-Assessment', *American Psychological Society* 5: 69–106.

Estlund, David (2008), *Democratic Authority* (Princeton, NJ: Princeton University Press).

Frankfurt, Harry (1969), 'Alternate Possibilities and Moral Responsibility', *Journal of Philosophy* 66: 829–39.

Fukuyama, Francis (1992), *The End of History and the Last Man* (London: Penguin Books).

Gardiner, Stephen (2011), *A Perfect Moral Storm* (New York: Oxford University Press).

Gigerenzer, Gerd (2008), *Rationality for Mortals* (New York: Oxford University Press).

Haidt, Jonathan (2003), 'The Moral Emotions', in R. J. Davidson, K. R. Scherer, and H. H. Goldsmith (eds.), *Handbook of Affective Sciences* (Oxford: Oxford University Press) 852–70.

Hamilton, Clive (2010), *Requiem for a Species* (London and Washington, DC: Earthscan).

Hardin, Garrett (1968), 'The Tragedy of the Commons', *Science* 162: 1243–8.

Hare, R. M. (1981), *Moral Thinking* (Oxford: Clarendon Press).

Harris, John (2011), 'Moral Enhancement and Freedom', *Bioethics* 21: 102–11.

Hart, H. L. A. (1955), 'Are There any Natural Rights', *Philosophical Review* 64: 175–91.

Hobbes, Thomas (1651), *De Cive*.

Hume, David (1739–40/1978), *A Treatise of Human Nature*, 2nd edn. (Oxford: Oxford University Press).

——(1777/1975), *Enquiries concerning Human Understanding and concerning the Principles of Morals*, 3rd edn. (Oxford: Oxford University Press).

Insel, T. R. and Fernald R. D. (2004), 'How the Brain Processes Social Information: Searching for the Social Brain', *Annual Review of Neuroscience* 27: 697–722.

Joyce, Richard (2006), *The Evolution of Morality* (Cambridge, MA: MIT Press).

Kahneman, Daniel and Tversky, Amos (eds.) (2000), *Choices, Values, and Frames* (Cambridge: Cambridge University Press).

Kamm, Frances (1996), *Morality, Mortality*, vol. II. (New York: Oxford University Press).

——(2007), *Intricate Ethics* (New York: Oxford University Press).

Kosfeld, M., Heinrichs, M., Zak, P. J., Fischbacher, U., and Fehr, E. (2005), 'Oxytocin Increases Trust in Humans', *Nature* 435(2): 673–6.

Locke, John (1690/1990), *Two Treatises of Government*, 2nd edn. (London: J. M. Dent & Sons).

Macrae, C. N. and Johnston, L. (1998), 'Help, I Need Somebody: Automatic Action and Inaction', *Social Cognition* 16: 400–17.

Martin, James (2006), *The Meaning of the 21st Century* (London: Eden Project Books).

Mill, J. S. (1859/1978), *On Liberty*, 2nd edn., ed. E. Rapaport (Indianapolis: Hackett).

——(1861), *Considerations on Representative Government*.

Mischel, Walter (1974), 'Cognitive Appraisals and Transformations in Self-Control', in Bernhard Weiner (ed.), *Cognitive Views of Human Motivation* (New York: Academic Press).

Moore, G. E. (1903), *Principia Ethica* (Cambridge: Cambridge University Press).

Nozick, Robert (1974), *Anarchy, State, and Utopia* (New York: Basic Books).

Parfit, Derek (1984), *Reasons and Persons* (Oxford: Clarendon Press).

Persson, Ingmar (1994), 'The Groundlessness of Natural Rights', *Utilitas* 6: 9–24.

——(2004), 'Two Act-Omission Paradoxes', *Proceedings of the Aristotelian Society* 104 (pt. 2).

——(2005), *The Retreat of Reason* (Oxford: Clarendon Press).

——(2007a), 'The Act-Omission Doctrine and Negative Rights', *The Journal of Value Inquiry* 41: 15–29.

——(2007b), 'A Defence of Extreme Egalitarianism', in N. Holtug and K. Lippert-Rasmussen (eds.), *Egalitarianism: New Essays on the Nature and Value of Equality* (Oxford: Clarendon Press).

——(2009), 'Rights and the Asymmetry Between Creating Good and Bad Lives', in Melinda Roberts and David Wasserman (eds.), *Harming Future Persons* (Dordrecht: Springer).

——and Savulescu, Julian (2005), 'McMahan on the Withdrawal of Life-Prolonging Aid', *Philosophical Books* 16: 11–22.

————(2008), 'The Perils of Cognitive Enhancement and the Urgent Imperative to Enhance the Moral Character of Humanity', *Journal of Applied Philosophy* 25: 162–76.

————2011, 'The Turn for Ultimate Harm: A Reply to Fenton', *Journal of Medical Ethics* 37: 441–4.

————(2011), 'Getting Moral Enhancement Right: The Desirability of Moral Enhancement', *Bioethics*.

Pinker, Steven (2011), *The Better Angels of Our Nature* (London: Allen Lane).

Posner, Richard (2004), *Catastrophe: Risk and Response* (New York: Oxford University Press).

Prinz, Jesse and Shaun Nichols (2010), 'Moral Emotions', in John Doris and The Moral Psychology Research Group (eds.), *The Moral Psychology Handbook* (Oxford: Oxford University Press).

Putnam, Robert (2007), 'E Pluribus Unum: Diversity and Community in the Twenty-first Century', *Scandinavian Political Studies* 30: 137–74.

Rachels, James (1975), 'Active and Passive Euthanasia', *New England Journal of Medicine* 292: 78–80.

Rampino, Michael (2008), 'Super-volcanism and Other Geophysical Processes of Catastrophic Import', in N. Bostrom and M. Ćirković (eds.), *Global Catastrophic Risks* (Oxford: Oxford University Press).

Rashdall, Hastings (1907), *The Theory of Good and Evil*, vol. I. (Oxford: Clarendon Press).

Rawls, John (1971), *A Theory of Justice* (Harvard: Harvard University Press).

Rees, Martin (2003), *Our Final Century* (London: William Heinemann).

Seitz, John (2008), *Global Issues*, 3rd edn. (Oxford: Blackwell).

Shearman, David and Smith, Joseph Wayne (2007), *The Climate Challenge and the Failure of Democracy* (Westport, CT: Praeger).

Singer, Peter (1993), *Practical Ethics*, 2nd edn. (Cambridge: Cambridge University Press).

Sober, Elliot and Sloan Wilson, David (1998), *Unto Others* (Cambridge, MA: Harvard University Press).

Stich, Stephen, Doris, J., and Roedder, E. (2010), 'Altruism', in John Doris and The Moral Psychology Research Group (eds.), *The Moral Psychology Handbook* (Oxford: Oxford University Press).

Sunstein, Cass (2007), *Worst-Case Scenarios* (Cambridge, MA: Harvard University Press).

Temkin, Larry (1996), 'A Continuum Argument for Intransitivity', *Philosophy and Public Affairs* 23: 175–210.

Thaler, Richard and Sunstein, Cass (2009), *Nudge* (London: Penguin).

Thomson, Judith (1990), *The Realm of Rights* (Cambridge, MA: Harvard University Press).

Tse, W. S. and Bond, A. J. (2002), Serotonergic Intervention Affects Both Social Dominance and Affiliative Behaviour, *Psychopharmacology* 161: 324–30.

Tuck, Richard (2008), *Free Riding* (Cambridge, MA: Harvard University Press).

Unger, Peter (1996), *Living High and Letting Die* (New York: Oxford University Press).

Veatch, Robert (1986), *The Foundations of Justice* (New York: Oxford University Press).

Waldron, Jeremy (1988), *The Right to Private Property* (Oxford: Clarendon Press).

——(2002), *God, Locke and Equality* (Cambridge: Cambridge University Press).

Wallace, B., Cesarini, D., Lichtenstein, P., and Johannesson, M. (2007), 'Heritability of Ultimatum Game Responder Behavior', *Proceedings of the National Academy of Sciences* 104(40): 15631–4.

Wilson, E. O. (2002), *The Future of Life* (London: Little Brown).

Wood, R. M., Rilling, J. K., Sanfey, A. G., Bhagwagar, Z., and Rogers, R. D. (2006), 'Effects of Tryptophan Depletion on the Performance of an Iterated Prisoner's Dilemma Game in Healthy Adults', *Neuropsychopharmacology* 31(5): 1075–84.

Yudkowski, Eliezer (2008), 'Cognitive Biases Potentially Affecting Judgement of Global Risks', in N. Bostrom and M. Ćirković (eds.), *Global Catastrophic Risks* (Oxford: Oxford University Press).

Zak, P., Kurzban, R., and Matzner, W. (2004), 'The Neurobiology of Trust', *Annals of the New York Academy of Sciences* 1032: 224–7.

Index

Printed in Poland
by Amazon Fulfillment
Poland Sp. z o.o., Wrocław